Florida State University Studies

NUMBER TWELVE

CHALLENGES TO LIBRARIANSHIP

Edited by
LOUIS SHORES

FLORIDA STATE UNIVERSITY

Tallahassee

1953

FLORIDA STATE UNIVERSITY STUDIES

Published under the Auspices
of
The Research Council
The Florida State University

EDITORIAL COMMITTEE

Mary Magginis, *Chairman*

Graydon S. DeLand Harold J. Humm

Weymouth T. Jordan Winthrop N. Kellogg

George Yost, Jr.

EDITOR

Weymouth T. Jordan

CONTENTS

INTRODUCTION: CHALLENGES TO LIBRARIANSHIP . . . 1
   Louis Shores

THE CHALLENGE OF INTERNATIONAL UNDERSTANDING . 13
   Dan Lacy

THE CHALLENGE OF CENSORSHIP 39
   Luther Evans

THE CHALLENGE OF MICROPHOTOGRAPHY 55
   Fremont Rider

LIBRARIANSHIP AND THE SCIENCES 69
   Charles Harvey Brown

THE CHALLENGE OF AUDIO-VISUAL MEDIA 93
   Edgar Dale

THE CHALLENGE OF SCHOOL LIBRARIANSHIP 107
   Frances Henne

THE CHALLENGE OF LIBRARY LITERATURE TO EDUCATION
      FOR LIBRARIANSHIP 125
   Louis Round Wilson

AN AMERICAN LIBRARIAN'S HERITAGE 141
   Wayne Shirley

FLORIDA STATE UNIVERSITY STUDIES
NUMBER TWELVE
Copyright 1953 by The Florida State University

CHALLENGES TO LIBRARIANSHIP*

LOUIS SHORES
Dean, Library School
Florida State University

1.

In the summer of 1952, after a year's inventory abroad and at home it was apparent that librarianship was confronted by a number of challenges with implications so deep that not only the profession, but scholarship at large, and indeed the fate of all mankind, could be affected.

These challenges were many and complex. But their direction was simple. Either libraries would provide that medium of communication essential to a one-world concept; or it would not and the dual-world struggle would continue. That was the way it appeared to some of us in 1952.

If somehow the next generation of librarians could be made aware of the over-all challenge to our profession, the history of the second half of the twentieth century might yet read better than the story of the first half. With this hope and conviction a series of eight lectures for the students of the Library School at Florida State University, was projected to be delivered at intervals during the academic year 1952-53. Each lecture was to identify a separate aspect of the over-all challenge and each lecturer was to be a member of the profession who had especially related himself to that aspect.

The lecture series was singularly successful from several standpoints. In the first place, the lecturers were unusually stimulating to the University community. In the second place,

*An introduction to the eight public lectures given at the Florida State University, Tallahassee, during the academic year 1952-1953.

each of the lecturers spent from several days to several weeks of residence on the campus, meeting, eating, and talking with students and faculty, thus preparing the background for the lecture effort. In the third place, since the lectures themselves were held outside the Library School (six of them in the Science Hall, and two in the Student Center Trophy Room) an extraordinary number of faculty and students from other disciplines, and especially from the Natural Sciences, as well as from the community, were attracted. And in the last place, the period of time for which each of the lecturers was detained after the lecture for questions and discussions, provided an evidence of the impact the challenge had had on the audience.

Identification of the eight separate challenges was in itself a challenge. Over all, librarianship was confronted by defiance on numerous fronts. It would therefore have been easy to extend the series by many more lectures.

Dominant in the planning, however, was the challenge of the world conflict. Possibly because this writer had just returned from a year in Europe and had previously spent several years in Asia and on other continents of the world, the challenge of the East-West struggle overshadowed all else. The issues raised by this war of ideas seemed to push librarians to the fore as men of destiny. With this in mind the eight professional challenges were selected.

2.

In Naples, Italy, the United States Information Center was fighting psychologically for the minds of man against the strong bid by a Soviet Book Center only a few doors down the street. And in the nearly 200 other communities outside the Iron Curtain the same battle was being repeated. Now this was American librarianship with overtones. This was a professional challenge of a different sort from that of the public library extension effort, stateside. It was evident that over there and perhaps increasingly over here librarians would have something more positive to contend with than mere inertia toward reading. Here was a foe of intellectual proportions prepared to outsell, out-maneuver, out-smart the whole system of acknowledged American library leadership. Here was a challenge to the principles of book selection, to the readers' advisory service, to indeed the whole American professional concept of dissemination and diffusion of knowledge, by a dynamic force opposed to us and determined to attract away from us our registered borrowers.

That we were professionally equal to this challenge our nearly 200 USIS centers all over the free world and beyond testified. We met the opposition's blue print for a better world with an unrestrained opportunity for free inquiry. Against their prescribed propoganda we directed the rich and unhampered best thought of all time. And we did this in a form that showed we understood the principles of communication. Because we in America had pioneered readability and audio-visual media.

This was psychological warfare and the weapons were the stuff that libraries are made of. This was the ideological war fought with the inevitable weapons of ideas. This was, indeed, the so-called "cold war" between East and West that now and then warmed to physical combat. But in the year 1952 it appeared to more than a minority of thinking individuals that mankind might at last have arrived of necessity at that level of mental maturity which would prefer psychological to physical combat.

To present the challenge of psychological warfare to the next generation of librarians we elected one of the generals of our Psychological Army contributed by the library profession. As head of the United States Department of State network of information centers Dan Lacy directed a vast and strategic operation. His own appreciation of the mission is indicated in his apt substitution for my challenge, "psychological warfare," of the term "international understanding."

"What lies ahead of us," he notes in an essay which must surely take its place as one of our professional classics, "is the most gigantic problem of conveying knowledge . . . in human history." For "the numerous channels of communication that unite the Western powers are blocked, impeded or constricted in their extension to Asia." These channels can be cleared by librarianship if the librarian is prepared to adapt his historic role of preserver and disseminator to a world-stage divided between haves and have-nots as far as the media-print, picture, cinema, radio are concerned. "Never before" as Mr. Lacy writes, "has the weight of the future hung so heavily on the labors of teachers and bookmen."

3.

But while this struggle was going on abroad all was not peace at home. Other challenges presented themselves to librarianship. There was the challenge of censorship—a frightened defense against a startling offense. Everywhere political and business voices were lifted to advocate meeting propaganda with propaganda, blue print with blue print, totalitarianism with totalitarianism. If the East censored the words of the West then the West must censor the words of the East. If books discussing the American way of life were not admitted to Soviet libraries then, of course, books on Marxism must be barred from Western libraries. American librarianship met this challenge with a Library Bill of Rights and with courageous statements of position by Library leaders.

What mark McCarthyism will leave on the future is uncertain. It may bring on George Orwell's "1984." A new Inquisition more horrible than the historic one may be in the making. But history will have on record that this challenge was met by various forces and institutions of freedom, and by none more resolutely than librarianship and libraries. And among the library leaders who spoke out in defense of freedom of inquiry none was so eloquent as the Librarian of Congress.

Perhaps it was that distinguished background in political science combined with the Texan's traditional courage and frankness that produced this keen observation about American sociological jitters in 1952. Writes Dr. Evans:

. . . the psychological unsettlement in which the American people find themselves today is primarily attributed to one enormous fact, namely, that they have more responsibility in the world than they know how to discharge.

The sadists of freedom are really cowards who are unwilling to live the American dream.

4.

In the year 1952, also, we were challenged by the "tidal wave of printed materials pouring into our research libraries." The mere problem of storing the never-ending torrent of researches pushed library architects to extremes of devices. That such space-saving inventions could be only temporary answers was proved by the regular doubling of library collections on the average of every sixteen years. The prospect of a Yale University Library in the year 2038 A.D. with a collection of over 200,000,000 volumes occupying 6,000 miles of shelving and requiring 750,000 catalog drawers to contain the necessary indexing defied the profession to produce another Melvil Dewey.

For some time now an increasing number of his colleagues have been convinced Fremont Rider is the answer to that challenge. It is doubtful if we have any one in our professional midst with more versatility. Publisher, author, inventor, librarian, known as his activities in these occupations are, they represent only a few of his lifetime pursuits. The magazines he edited were the newstands' best sellers of the first years of this century. As investigator no problem was beyond his curiosity. Witness his early study of life after death. As inventor, no obstacle, regardless of its scope, prevented an original and often startling proposal. Recall his resolve of the great dilemma of world organization. As librarian the nimbleness of his mind often left the rest of us standing behind. How I recall chairmaning the first committee on classification and pay plans for institutions of higher education. All day long we, the committee, padded laboriously over meticulous details. In the middle of the night and by himself Fremont Rider would boldly and magnificently create a whole that gathered the minutiae into a masterpiece.

That sort of a mind was librarianship's answer to the challenge of the printed tidal wave. And that sort of a mind produced the microcard, which if still challenged as the best of the micro texts for all purposes, is nevertheless moving toward that position. And regardless of that point the microcard is at least an answer to the challenge of storage and rapid dissemination which confronts librarianship.

For as Dr. Rider writes, "It is the immediate accessibility of the texts that they desire that is to the vast majority of scholars, the only *sine qua non* of library service."

5.

The cause of much of this research cavalcade was the natural sciences. By 1952 the humanities and humanistic researches were the forgotten members of the academic family. Mankind had almost turned its back on an approach to reality which appeared to be lacking in speed, glamour, or material advantage. Young men and young women, too, captivated by Atom-splitting, comfort-promoting gadgets, and big money were turning to science in increasing numbers. But librarianship continued to draw heavily from the humanities, and to a lesser extent from the social sciences.

Here was a challenge. Could this low-paying profession of librarianship attract members of the high-paying scientific society? Or could librarians with humanistic backgrounds reorient themselves sufficiently for the method and material of science to serve adequately the compelling and staccato needs of the way on which mankind now wagered its future? That was the challenge.

For the needs were urgent. In 1952, it has been estimated that not fewer than "a million useful scientific articles are published yearly in some 50,000 scientific journals. . . ." The challenge to librarianship was to disseminate these researches to the point of critical need on time so that the interval between discovery and application might be eliminated. In the year 1952 librarianship was still struggling with the problems of bibliographic organization, striving vainly to accelerate devices for dissemination to match the overwhelming pace of production.

This led Charles Harvey Brown, our leading science bibliographer, and himself that rare librarian who was first a mathematician and later an enthusiastic student of the literatures of the natural sciences to observe that librarians are not serving scientific research adequately, because the profession has drawn overwhelmingly from the Humanities, and the Humanistic approach for research is quite different from the method of Science.

"A somewhat different concept of a library is needed by librarians," concluded Dr. Brown, who for over a quarter of a century provided the stimulation to professional organization by librarians collectively, and inspiration for professional growth to librarians, individually. His essay will record for the future that a profession rooted in the humanities extended its branches into the sciences in time to support exploration of this approach to reality.

6.

Are educators and psychologists opposed to the printed word as a medium of communication? The inroads of so-called audio-visual media upon readers' time led many critics, including Joseph Wood Krutch to see a menace to books in radio, film and television. Here is a challenge to librarians of no mean proportion.

It seemed fitting that the educator whose first notable contributions were in the field of readability and his second in audio-visual media should take up this challenge especially in view of his philosophical belief, a belief shared and sponsored by the Florida State University Library School, that there is a unity in the mission of all media of communications and that the library is strategically equipped to provide the unifying vehicle through which those blocked channels Mr. Lacy describes can be opened.

In his essay Dr. Dale has stated better than any one before the relationship among the various media and the library's potential role. He has indeed produced the slogan of greatest possible value for this cold war world: "Your Library Has the Best Ideas in the World."

How to transmit these ideas so that they reach all mankind at the farthest points from the United States in physical and psychological distance seemed a challenge of stature for librarianship in 1952 and one which might turn the tide for a one-world victory. To Dr. Dale there is no one medium. There is a world of media in which the "printed word is still the most generally efficient and effective method of conveying thought or information ever invented by man, and that over the largest of all fields a hundred words is often worth a thousand pictures."

At the same time the librarian is confronted by the facts that "about half of the adults in this world cannot read or write . . . and that the average adult in this country has about nine years of education."

Of course we should bring the whole world up to using the most efficient medium in the world. But while we are doing this shall we keep the world divided by living half informed and half uninformed? Or shall we turn to other media—film, filmstrip, recording—that will reach the illiterate right now?

The challenge to librarianship is to display through television in every home those best ideas in the world which the library has.

7.

If you want adults who can read you must provide reading opportunities for children. This is a challenge not to school librarians alone but to the whole profession. The University librarian who shuts himself out from the existence of school libraries has only himself to blame for inadequate library appreciation in his academic community. The public librarian who ignores school libraries must hold himself responsible for the non-borrowers in his community. Problems of school librarianship are the foundations of half-a-world of adult illiteracy.

That challenge is vividly posed by Dr. Henne who has been in the vanguard of school library planning. To this overall challenge she adds some startling subordinates. One of these is the challenge to provide library opportunities in the elementary school. Another is the dare to change over the present school library into a materials center. A third is the gauntlet fling for librarians on the defensive about non-book media to become versatile with motion picture projectors and tape recorders and reasonably conversant in the literature of these media.

There are three more challenges in school librarianship but all six add up to the preparation of a better next generation. As Dr. Henne writes "To all librarians, not just to school librarians, belongs the major challenge of school librarianship; for this challenge calls upon us as citizens as well as librarians, and cuts across the segments of specialized professional interests."

8.

In 1923 our professional literature was inconsiderable; in 1953 it is seriously considerable.

Its impact on professional education for librarianship has been enriching.

A review of the literature on librarianship reveals trends in emphases. At one period when the librarian was primarily a bookman the emphasis was on the humanistic. At another time when librarians became absorbed in administration our professional classics took their inspiration from business. In the last two decades librarianship has been influenced heavily by the social and natural sciences and this influence has manifested itself in quantitative measures, in surveys and questionaires, in an effort to emulate what science calls the objective approach.

These various lines in our professional writing Dr. Wilson ably traces because he himself has had such a major part in the last half century of library development. Although he modestly refrains from naming any of his own works while citing the writing of several of his colleagues as "classics," there can be no doubt among any of us who know our literature at all that certainly the *Geography of Reading* and possibly one or two others of his works would rank in any professional award.

The challenge to the new generation of librarians is explicit. "These are the materials which you must master if you are to be fully informed about how the graphic records of man's past and present can be made to minister effectively to his present and future." What the new generation takes from the present professional library to add a new shelf may well affect ultimately the success with which librarianship meets the overall world challenge.

9.

A positive answer to the question that confronts a divided world is offered by librarianship in its Heritage of America program. In it can be found the best of mankind's best ideas —dignity of the individual, cooperative social planning by free individuals, climate for individual initiative and enterprise, Christian brotherhood of man. If we could but appreciate this Heritage as the cause rather than the result of industrial and material leadership we could help the world save itself from threatening disaster.

Here is a challenge to out-challenge all challenges. Can librarianship rise to the supreme heights of its mission? Have we the imagination to turn colorless techniques into colorful services? Can we so present this wonderful heritage of free men to hungry peoples all over the world so as to save their birthright?

As Dean Shirley points out there are at least two of our talents which may act as obstacles. "The first is our love of gadgetry. . . . The second is our dreadful professional terminology." Neither contribution is really as effective on a world scale as it is in the narrow professional circles.

These weaknesses, however, are less than our strengths. "One great strength is our belief in the value of personality." Another is our faith in the organized library movement. A third is our dedication to cooperation. But above all is our missionary devotion to libraries as something "good in the sense of being counteracting forces to the evils which affect mankind."

Dean Shirley modestly disclaims any attempt to formulate

a philosophy of librarianship but in his commitment to these four beliefs he has designed both a defense and an offense against the negative forces which periodically in history confront mankind with the threat of chaos.

10.

In the pages that follow, these eight challenges are identified for 1952. How successfully they will be met, the next generation and the next must appraise. It is the hope of the contributors that the librarian classes of 1953 all over the world will read these eight essays now and again in 1963 and once more in 1973 and rate the previous generation on their foresight.

To all the contributors—lecturers, discussants, faculty and students of the Library School, and faculty and colleagues of the University, and to the Research Council and Editorial Committee of the University Studies this final paragraph of thanks is written.

THE CHALLENGE OF INTERNATIONAL UNDERSTANDING*

DAN LACY

*Director, Information Center Service
United States Department of State*

1.

Among the most frequently and least precisely used expressions of our time is the phrase "one world." We normally employ it in a moral or hortatory rather than in a descriptive sense; that is, when we say the world is one, we mean not that it is, but that people ought to behave as though it were. Even in that hortatory sense, however, we are generally so vague that we do not give our hopes a precise shape and meaning. Because the problems of international communication and the role of books and libraries in their solution are so intimately related to this concept of the unity of the world, it will be necessary for us at the beginning to make some exploration of its meaning, or rather of its meanings, because they are many.

2.

In the only important sense in which the world is still truly one, it has been one for a long time. As long ago as the end of the fifteenth and the beginning of the sixteenth century the maritime nations of Western Europe had achieved such an organization of resources as to be able to extend their power beyond the European peninsula. The increase of wealth that came from their control of the American continents and the superior forms of political and military organization developed in the seventeenth and eighteenth centuries enabled them to extend their dominion over most of coastal Asia, while the Russian branch of European civilization spread over the long reaches of Siberia.

The already nearly world-wide control of the European powers and their descendants overseas was enormously

*A public lecture given at Florida State University, Tallahassee, November 18, 1952.

strengthened by their development of steam as a source of power and the growth of a resulting economy based on the iron and coal that they alone possessed in abundance. The new industrial civilization of the nineteenth century gave these powers a previously undreamed of superiority of strength and a mobility that could extend to the ends of the earth. The Roman Empire could maintain over its barbarian enemies only the uneasy superiority of organization and discipline; by the mid-nineteenth century the industrial nations had achieved power beyond any menace that could ever be offered by non-industrial peoples. Their control was quickly extended and consolidated, and with the completion of the partition of Africa in the latter half of the nineteenth century the world had become what it will doubtless always remain: one arena of power. Never hereafter could any people carry out its destiny in remote safety from the principal centers of power. Never again would two contemporary empires, like the Chinese and Roman, or like the Indian and Spanish of the sixteenth century, be able to maintain their parallel courses independently of each other's existence. There could hereafter be but one power system in which every people must somehow find a place.

But by 1900 the world had become something more than one arena; in a sense, a very partial and imperfect sense, it had become one polity and one economy. The political unity, or more precisely, unity of political control, found expression in no formal organs. Though there was a generally observed, if limited, body of international law, there was no world government. But a loose concert of Western powers was able to assert an effective control over the entire earth. A majority of the world's population and resources was formerly under the control of one or another of them, and even those non-industrialized countries that were nominally independent were in fact closely constrained in the exercise of their sovereignty. The progressive limitations on China's political freedom of action imposed by the concert of Western powers constitute a case in point. If in spite of its internal political differences we may think of the West as a somewhat loose political unity, it had succeeded by that date in subjecting to that unity the rest of the world.

Somewhat similarly, the Western capitalistic industrial and commercial economy had spread itself over the entire world in the sense that raw materials flowed to its factories from every country, its products found markets everywhere, the patterns of economic activity in all the non-Western countries were increasingly determined by the needs of that economy, and the regulation of the entire economy was achieved by a calculus of prices in a few markets in which the products and buyers of all the world met. The lives of the half-savage worker chopping drainage channels in a guayule tree in the Amazon, of the Chinese peasant digging for ginger root, of the Bolivian Inca mining tin were all shaped by their participation in an economy ruled by the financial centers of the West. Only in increasingly constricted and primitive areas did separate local economies persist that did not contribute to or draw from the world market.

Moreover, within itself the West had achieved or maintained a certain measure of philosophic unity. In diverse forms the Western nations shared a common religious belief; they were in fact in an earlier day often referred to collectively as "Christendom." A common metaphysics and epistemology had been formed by the seventeenth century development of Platonic and Aristotelian systems. Their languages had been derived from a common source and possessed a marked similarity of syntax and psychological structure. A common body of scientific knowledge enlightened, as a common esthetic heritage enriched, their lives. Among themselves, and in spite of all their complex differences, Westerners could communicate.

3.

Thus by the beginning of our century the world had become one theater of history, all of whose people were woven together in the web of one political and economic order. And this order in turn was formed and guided by the values and the knowledge and skills of one Western culture.

Though all men had a place within this order and though the lives of all were shaped by it, few participated in it in the sense of helping to make its political and economic decisions, enjoying the rewards of its previously undreamed of productivity, or sharing the highly developed body of knowledge and ideas that underlay it. Hundreds of millions of men throughout the world, but especially in Asia, lived out their lives in a misery in no way lightened by the Western industrial order. Perhaps to most of them its coming meant only that their labors were now performed and their lives governed as other men willed, with a consequent disintegration of their own institutions and a debasement of their own dignity.

However, the very unequal sharing of its benefits among the millions who came under its control should blind no one to the contributions of that Western order to the world. First, its skill at production, developed out of its science and its gift for social organization, achieved an outpouring of goods and a mastery over nature never before conceived. Though it is still a gross exaggeration even in 1953 to say that we can produce enough for all, it is true to say that Western science and industry for the first time in all the agony of human history made it possible for a very considerable portion of the human race to live in comfort and relative plenty. Second, the development of its culture was based on a conception of individual freedom of belief, inquiry, and speech never before so widely or so deeply held. Third, though singularly blind to its extension to others (few of the men who proclaimed that "all men are created equal" ever thought of their own slaves in this way) nevertheless Western culture developed within itself a humane and democratic ethos that promised a nobler and richer role for individual men than had ever before been offered by any society. For all its monstrous inequities, no other civilization has achieved so much or held out so fair a hope for mankind as the Western civilization that only yesterday ruled the world.

4.

The world order based on that civilization has now collapsed. The disorganization that followed World War I became far more general and complete after World War II. The world has lost the sense of philosophic unity and common purpose that guided Christendom. The political control over non-Western powers has been withdrawn or abandoned or overthrown. The smooth flow of materials and goods in a largely autonomous economy has been disrupted, and the economy itself threatens to disintegrate into a congeries of separate national economies.

The consequent chaos surrounds us everywhere. Even within most of the Western states internal stress and disorganization are evident. Between the Communist world and the free world there now remain no community of purpose or ideas, almost no economic relationship, and scarcely any meaningful political relationship except the cold fear of each other's strength. The agony of Asian awakening, for all of its increasingly hopeful promise of the future, has now reached only that point at which a new order is beginning to emerge from the collapse of the old. This state is symbolized by the impasse on Iranian oil, in which the Iranians are unwilling to continue the old economic order and are not yet able to create a new, with a consequent paralysis of economic activity and a possibly impending disintegration of political order.

It is perhaps beyond our task to explore the reasons for the decline and fall of this world order which reached its apogee at the turn of the century; but some of the causes are obvious and are relevant to our purposes:

1. In the first place, that order had never achieved an entire unity within itself. The skeptical rationalism on which it was founded destroyed faith faster than it created it; its democratic and humane values were never fully accepted; its atomistic individualism was never fully satisfying; and even within the centers of western power most men, like nearly all men outside the West, felt disfranchised and excluded from both participation and benefit. The consequence was the rise of dissident, embittered, and totalitarian movements like fascism and communism which rent the unity of purpose of the West itself.

2. The massive civil wars within the West, which we know as the two World Wars, and the menace of a third have destroyed the wealth and confused and enfeebled the will of the European powers.

3. The moral principles developed within Western culture were turned upon the West's relation to the other areas on which it had imposed its control, with the result that the political and economic exploitation of other countries became repugnant to the West.

4. Finally, what had become repugnant to the West became intolerable to the East, and the Near Eastern and Asian nations simply threw off the weakened and now half-hearted dominance of the West.

5.

And so we see repeated before our eyes the vast and tragic drama which has several times before altered the massive course of history itself—the enfeeblement of the organizing principle that has held a great civilization together and the resultant disintegration of its unity.

In the past, such situations have led to epochs of anarchy like that which followed the collapse of the Roman Empire. The economic life of the mass of their citizens having come but a little way from barbarism, such civilizations could relapse into a primitive state as civilization today cannot. The population of the world approximately trebled in the century and a quarter of Western abundance following the Napoleonic wars, and became distributed about the earth's surface in a highly asymmetrical pattern in accord with the operations of a world economy. Great cities of millions of persons grew up whose life can be sustained from day to day only through the swift and orderly functioning of a vast economic network. Anarchy cannot be endured. The life, not of our civilization alone, but of our very selves, of men all over the world, depends on a stable, orderly, and relative peaceful economy.

Let me repeat: anarchy will not be tolerated. If order is not achieved, it will be imposed. A brutal and totalitarian force, sharing nothing of the West except its technology, stands ready to enforce its rule over every area where chaos admits it. Witness the collapse of the Chinese government and economy and the swift entry of Communism. That same threat exists everywhere there is instability, and its agents do everything in their power to bring about the collapse that will give them their opportunity.

6.

The alternatives before our civilization thus are clear. World order will be restored. It will be a voluntary world order in which free nations and men voluntarily collaborate, or it will be an imposed and totalitarian order under which the sleet-gray years ahead can offer only the faceless extinction of our hopes.

It should be obvious from even so summary a resumé that the restoration of a stable order embracing as much of the world as possible is the greatest problem of public policy of our time. Since it is beyond any reasonable hope that such an order can within the predictable future be made to embrace Russia or the areas it controls, the problem becomes one primarily of reintegrating the West and Asia (including the Near East) on a basis that will command the assent of the Eastern peoples. Precisely because any stable new political and economic relationship between the West and Asia must be one accepted freely and with understanding by Asians, it must be based on a far wider and more accurate comprehension by Asians of the West than now exists and on a wider participation by them in the values and techniques of Western civilization. Particularly is this true with respect to the United States, less known in Eastern areas than France or Great Britain but now the center and the symbol of Western strength.

Let us try to see what this requires in more concrete terms. Most obviously of all it requires that the Asian and the Near Eastern areas become masters of the complex technical skills developed by Western civilization. Without that they cannot direct an industrial economy or achieve the revolutionary increases in productivity that are necessary for a share in the material well-being this order must produce. This involves far more than industrial and agricultural technology. Medical knowledge and the other applications of Western science are equally necessary to a share in a better life. Moreover, it will be necessary to share also in the fundamental theoretic knowledge and in the related philosophical outlooks that underlie these achievements. And, finally, the techniques of social, economic, and political organization and their underlying social sciences are requisite to the effective direction and control of a modern economy.

(Let me insert here that it is obvious that there is a great deal that the West needs to learn from and about Asia and the Near East both in order to conduct its relations with those areas with a more informed intelligence and to benefit from the rich moral and spiritual insights of their ancient civilizations. But here the problem is one of the will to learn rather than of the means of communication, and lies beyond the scope of this paper.)

What lies before us is the most gigantic problem of conveying knowledge, of education, if you will, in human history. Conceive of this infinitely complex and powerful body of knowledge and theory which constitutes the heart—the universally valid portion—of Western civilization and which has until the last two or three generations been the possession of a small elite even within our own civilization. Consider what a gigantic effort, occupying the recent decades, it has been to extend this to the major part of our own group, and yet how necessary that educational effort has been before the majority of Americans and other Westerners could fully share in our society as producers, as consumers, and citizens. Consider too with what staggering speed that body of knowledge is multiplying its scope and complexity so that for all our educational effort we are at a loss even within the United States to know how we can realistically convey some understanding of the content of modern science and thought to our children.

It is to participation in this unbelievably rich and intricate intellectual realm that we seek at one time to admit a population of a billion and a half who must have its knowledge as their franchise of membership in the world we must create. And at the heels of this effort runs the hot breath of catastrophe itself.

7.

It is clear that if we are to do this there must be a radical transformation and enlargement of our means of communication with Asians. All the numerous channels of communication that unite the Western powers are blocked, impeded, or constricted in their extension to Asia. Travel between the United States and Asia is negligible as compared to that between Europe and the United States. There are in Asia few radio receivers and fewer cinemas. In the United States there are 620 radios to every thousand persons, and almost everywhere each set can receive the programs of several stations and national networks. Almost as well supplied quantitatively and perhaps better qualitatively are the major countries of Europe, most of which average about one receiver to a family. In Iran and China there are three sets to a thousand people: in India and Indonesia one; in Burma one set serves 1700 people. And the programs they can receive are limited in number, time, and quality. Nearly ninety per cent of all television sets are in the United States, and substantially all the rest are in Europe. In the United States there are seventy-eight cinema seats per thousand people, a figure exceeded in Belgium, Italy, Sweden, and Great Britain and approached by most other European countries, as compared with an average of less than five per thousand in Asia and as few as one per thousand in several individual Asian countries. In the United States 354 issues of daily newspapers serve each thousand people, a figure approached by most of Europe and exceeded in Great Britain and Scandinavia. In India six issues, in Burma five, in Indonesia four, in Pakistan two issues serve each thousand. When the content and volume of the papers is considered, the contrast is even greater. An American newspaper averages twenty to forty pages, a European eight to sixteen, an Asian two to six. The United States consumes over thirty-three kilograms of newsprint a year a person; India, less than one.

Few Western, particularly few American, books are available in Asia. Currency restrictions bar them from many countries, and the market is usually too limited to invite major promotional efforts of American publishers. Few have the means, even when they can obtain dollars, to buy American books, which are extremely expensive abroad.

Language differences impose a barrier to all communication with the West. Hundreds of millions of Asians are imprisoned in languages into which no important part of modern science and Western thought has been translated. Illiteracy compounds this difficulty, for most cannot read their own languages. Perhaps an even more formidable barrier than those set up by language and illiteracy is created by differences in cultural background, which make difficult the comprehension and use of those vehicles of communication that are available. Music, films, and books produced for Western audiences seldom convey ideas in terms readily comprehensible in Asia. Many technical works are simply not applicable in the Asian physical and cultural environment.

But the problem is by no means solely that of conveying a body of knowledge and ideas *to* another country; it involves equally the dissemination of that knowledge and those ideas within the country receiving them. It is obvious that American or other Western films and radio programs, American teachers, and American books can serve only as a means of initial entry. In the United States knowledge and ideas from abroad can achieve currency only as they become incorporated in American books or books translated and published here, repeated in American newspapers and magazines, broadcast over domestic radio stations and taught in American schools. The French or British or Italian book or teacher from which the idea or information has been derived will have served an indispensable purpose but a futile one unless the message is picked up and disseminated through our own channels. It is so in other countries as well, and though we may send abroad American books by the thousands, they will achieve their purpose only as their content is ultimately reflected in local publications.

The poverty of these local channels gravely accentuates the whole problem of communication in Asia. Not only the media we have mentioned, but schools, libraries, radio networks, and press services are for the most part in very early stages of development, without resources to reach the majority of the people, and incapable of carrying the heavy traffic of communication that is required.

The pattern of communication between the U. S. and Asia that does take place through these constricted channels is shaped by the opportunity for profit and by certain immediate American and Asian governmental ends. For example, many at least of the American films, books, and magazines that can be sold profitably abroad are likely to be cheap and sensational with a low or negative communication value. Asian governments in general feel able to support or subsidize only those areas of communication that immediately serve certain ends of economic and social development. Western governments, including ours, have in general subsidized only those areas of information that serve certain economic and political ends. In consequence, in most Asian countries, available American books tend not only to be few in number but also to be either of inferior quality or specially devoted to technical or political ends.

I hope that you will forgive me for having taken so long to arrive at last at the point at which we can begin specifically to discuss the role of books and libraries. But it seemed necessary first to try to define in some detail the overwhelming job —so much greater than is conveyed by the vague phrase "international understanding"—that must be done, and the very nearly insuperable impediments to its accomplishment.

In this task books, of course, play a major and indispensable part, and for two reasons. One is that, though other media have proved to be extremely useful auxiliaries, books are today, as they have been since Gutenberg, the only practical means of transmitting a complex body of knowledge and ideas. Only books provide the enduring, extensive, diverse medium, at the command of its users, that is required. They are the universal instruments of learning, abroad as well as here. When we speak of transmitting to another culture the intellectual content of Western civilization, books are the vessels in which it must be conveyed.

The second reason is that only in the case of books will economic and technological factors permit a rapid enlargement of the pattern of communication we have described. Large-scale extensions of other media, such as radio, films, newspapers, and schools require either heavy capital investment in facilities or long-range changes in the social patterns of the countries concerned. The low unit cost of books and the fact that their reasonably effective use requires no elaborate institutional or technical substructure could make possible a relatively easy and immediate improvement of the quality, expansion of the volume, and adjustment of the emphases of communication through this medium. Books are the quickest and cheapest way to begin to deal effectively with the enormous task we have described.

8.

Let us examine first what are the specific obstacles to the use of books as a vehicle of international communication. To some of these we have already referred in discussing the general impediments to East-West communication:

1. A major difficulty is the problem of monetary exchange. Almost all foreign governments lack dollars and must dole out those they receive in order to permit the importation of necessities from the United States. The possibility of importing American books thus depends on the policy of the local government and the current circumstances of trade. These vary widely. In Israel, for example, no dollars are made available by the Israeli government for the importation of books; in India at the opposite extreme a general license permits importers of books to use as many dollars as they can get for this purpose. In most countries dollar licenses are made available for necessary scientific and technical books but for little else. Even, as in India, where licenses are granted freely, the importer may still have to find his own dollars. Fortunately, the shortages of pounds and francs in Asia, though they exist, are not so acute, and a considerable flow of British and French books is possible. Unfortunately, there is no shortage at all of rubles and Russian books find no currency obstacles.

2. A second difficulty is price. American books are expensive to begin with. When they are translated into foreign currencies at rates of exchange that tend to exaggerate the purchasing power of the dollar, they may be priced out of the local market altogether. A five-dollar American book, priced in local currencies, may cost a week's wages of an Asian clerk. In most Asian markets hard-cover American books, with the exception of those that serve as the tools of a profession—like medical books—can be bought only by a tiny minority. European books, more cheaply manufactured and sold at a less unfavorable exchange rate, are cheaper; subsidized Russian books are the cheapest of all.

3. A third difficulty is that long-standing trade arrangements reserve to British publishers the rights to most popular American books in the British Commonwealth area, including India, Pakistan, Ceylon, and Burma. When a corresponding British edition is brought out simultaneously with the American and marketed in the area no problem is presented; but such agreements may bar from this crucial area inexpensive American reprints of books for which no corresponding British reprint has appeared.

4. A fourth difficulty resides in the fact that in many other areas of the Near East and Asia local legislation does not recognize copyrights in translations of American or other books. This freedom to issue translations has been insisted on by the governments of those countries precisely in order to protect their ability to draw from the reservoirs of Western knowledge to meet their national needs; but by denying protection to the publishers, foreign or domestic, who may wish to bring out translations, it probably has an opposite effect.

5. We have mentioned the barrier of language. It is a matter of the utmost good fortune that a very high proportion of the intellectual leaders of the Near East and Asia read English. Especially is this true in those countries—India, Pakistan, Ceylon, Burma, the Malay States, and the Philippines—that have been a part of the British or the American commonwealths. English is widely known in Egypt as well, French throughout the Near East and in Indo-China, and Dutch in Indonesia. Books in the Western languages, and particularly in English, are hence effective in the initial task of providing an entry for a body of knowledge *into* a country. But to achieve the ultimate purpose of a widespread dissemination within each country, no flow of Western books, however large, can suffice; the indispensable need is for locally produced books in vernacular tongues.

6. The sixth obstacle to the use of Western books in the Near East and Asia is the scarcity of books suitable for local situations and local audience. The Asian market is not large enough to evoke the production of American or other Western books prepared with its particular needs in view. The American books we can draw on for use or sale in Asia were written with the interests, needs, and backgrounds of American readers in mind. In certain fields, such as mathematics and the pure sciences, this presents no problem. But even the simplest account of American history, politics, or economics is likely to take for granted information which very few Asians have. Government pamphlets on infant care written for use even in remote rural areas of this country assume the availability of canned milk, nursing bottles, electricity, absorbent cotton, and mineral oil—not to mention diapers—which are likely to be rare or unheard of in most of the areas with which we are concerned. Agricultural books of the West do not deal with the crops, the soils, the pests or the climate encountered in the East. Even the most purely theoretical works on economics, political science, and sociology written in the West consciously or unconsciously embody assumptions drawn from Western experience and are hence to this degree inapplicable in an Eastern environment. Again it is obvious that Western books can introduce ideas and knowledge into Eastern countries, but that the effective dissemination of information requires its local transmutation.

7. In view of these considerations the inadequacy of local facilities for the publication of books and for their dissemination to the public becomes one of the most important obstacles of all to the effective use of books. Throughout the Near East and Asia (I am excluding here, as in most parts of this paper, Japan in view of the degree to which it has already absorbed many aspects of Western civilization), publishing as it is known in Western Europe or the United States hardly exists. In Egypt, Pakistan, India, Indonesia, and the Philippines there are book publishers of sorts; but their capital, their resources for translation, editing, manufacture, and promotion are very small. Even in so enormous a country and so intelligent a country as India, 5,000 copies of a book is a large edition; few books are published at all; and those that are, are likely to be slight in size and content. In the other Near Eastern and Asian countries there is scarcely any organized, professional book publication.

8. Commercial book distribution, of local or Western books, is similarly limited except in the large cities. It is substantially impossible to sell a large edition of any book throughout the area.

9. Finally, libraries capable of serving as an effective channel for the dissemination of books to the public hardly exist. There are national libraries in most Asian countries, but none of them serves as an effective

point of entry for Western ideas and knowledge into the intellectual life of its country; indeed, none of them has funds for any significant purchases of Western books. A few, such as those of Turkey, Egypt, the Lebanon, India, and the Philippines, afford promise of vitality, but even these are understandably primarily concerned with the preservation of their own cultural patrimony rather than with the introduction of elements from other cultures. More useful for this purpose are the university libraries, which are located frequently in centers of great intellectual ferment and eager exploration of Western knowledge. Few of these libraries are supported with any adequacy, however; and their buildings and collections are likely to be as small as the enthusiasm and purpose of their librarians are high. Of public libraries capable of reaching the generality of literate men and women there are now almost none.

9.

This is a depressing picture; but I think we can draw real pride and hope from a survey of what is being done to enlarge the effectiveness of books in this enormous task of communication. It is obvious that measures of two kinds are required: one group aimed at helping in the initial transplantation of ideas and knowledge, the other at helping in their adaptation and dissemination within the Asian countries.

Among the first group of measures—those aimed at getting information *into* the East—we may mention efforts to increase the commercial availability of American and other Western scholarly books; the services of American and other Western libraries in the area; and programs to enlarge the holdings and reinforce the competence of university and other research libraries in the area.

Efforts toward the stimulation of the commercial flow of scholarly and technical books have largely been devoted to eliminating or reducing currency problems. UNESCO has approached this through the use of its now well known "book coupons," subsequently extended in their application to include educational films and scientific equipment. These coupons are sold by UNESCO for francs or other "soft" currencies but may be used by the purchaser in buying books from a "hard" currency country, since UNESCO is prepared to redeem them in dollars or other "hard" currencies. UNESCO is enabled to do this in part because a major part of its receipts are in hard currencies; but most of its operations are in soft-currency countries and can be financed with soft currencies, and in part because an increasing number of American libraries use coupons bought with dollars to pay for their foreign purchases. Well over $2,000,000 of these coupons have been issued, primarily to Asian countries. Though they have been used for purchases from a number of countries, over two-thirds of those redeemed have been used to buy American books or other educational materials. Currently this scheme makes possible the flow of about $50,000 worth of materials a month. This is a device that could solve all the currency problems involved if UNESCO had the financial resources to permit its full-scale utilization; but the sums available are little more than trivial in relation to needs.

A second and potentially much larger means to the same end is the Informational Media Guaranty Program of this government. Under this program the United States Government under certain conditions can redeem for dollars, the receipts in foreign currencies of publishers or exporters of books, newspapers, magazines, films and other informational media "consistent with the national interest of the United States." Until the summer of 1952 this program was administered by the Mutual Security Administration and until a year ago exports only to the Western European countries participating in the old ECA program could be covered. Since the passage of the Mutual Security Act of 1951, however, the program has been eligible for extension to most Asian and Near Eastern countries, and it is now administered by the Information Center Service of the State Department in the context of the general information program. Its extension, however, requires the conclusion of an agreement with each country to which it applies, and that country subsequently has the right of approval over the particular projects carried on under the program. So far, such agreements have been reached only with Israel and the Philippines within the area with which we are concerned, and circumstances have delayed the effective application of the Philippine program. We are now, however, actively pushing negotiations in this area, and I hope that this program can soon be extended to most of those Eastern countries in which it is needed. Since the law authorizes the conversion of up to $10,000,000 of foreign currency a year, it is obvious that this is potentially a major contribution to the solution of the problem.

The Eastern nations themselves, through the assignment to book imports of a share of their precious reserve of dollars, have done much to ease though not yet to solve the problem.

UNESCO has taken another important step through the international agreement prepared under its auspices on the Importation of Educational, Scientific and Cultural Materials. This Agreement was drafted by a committee of experts and adopted by the Fifth General Conference of UNESCO in July 1950 and came into effect as among the signatory countries on May 21, 1952. In the area of our concern, Cambodia, Ceylon, Egypt, Israel, Laos, Pakistan, and Thailand have ratified the agreement and in addition Afghanistan, China, Iran, and the Philippines have signed it. In spite of a number of concessions made to it, the United States unhappily has not, though most other major Western powers have. This Agreement obligates its adherents to exempt all printed books from customs duties and other importation charges and to grant foreign exchange and import licenses for books being imported by libraries and research institutions, for official publications, and for certain other classes.

It has been possible to do very little directly to reduce the price of books exported from the United States. Any really major reduction, in view of the cost structure of the American publishing industry, can come only from inexpensive reprinting in paper-bound format. This, again, is practicable only for books with very large potential sales, far larger than can be even approached by the foreign market. This means that at present only those American books can be produced in inexpensive editions for sale abroad for which such editions are justified by the American market. It would be highly desirable if the Government were able to co-operate with American publishers to reduce the price of exported American books, but the legal and policy problems involved have not yet been solved. I do believe, however, that there has now been devised a means which will enable a number of books to be brought out in cheap reprints for overseas use without regard to the American market.

Let me here also pay tribute to the many American publishers who, bearing a keen sense of responsibility for the solution of this problem have expended on the promotion of American books in the East sums of money and effort out of proportion to any possible return from the present market.

A second major instrument, in addition to the sale of American and other Western books, has been the operation by the United States and by certain other countries of libraries abroad. The largest effort has been that of the United States. Through its International Information Center Service the State Department operates nearly two hundred American libraries abroad, of which 115 are in Asia and the Near East. These libraries are small, having from 2500 to 25,000 volumes, from 50 to 450 periodical subscriptions, and from 2 or 3 to 25 or 30 employees. They can present a broad picture of Western thought in the natural and social sciences as reflected in American books and journals. They reach a very large group; last year the Asian and Near Eastern libraries alone were visited by 9,500,000 persons and loaned 3,500,000 books. They are especially effective in transmitting knowledge about the government and economy of the United States itself. But obviously they cannot be research libraries. Equally obviously, eight little libraries each of less than 10,000 volumes cannot hope to serve as an effective contact for broad fields of knowledge between the West and the hundreds of millions of Indians, and the disproportion of size and task is almost equally great elsewhere. Somewhat similar libraries, but smaller, far fewer, and more restricted in their audience, are maintained by the British and French through semi-official organizations.

In addition, one should call attention to the libraries of colleges and universities maintained by the Western powers under official or religious auspices, of which the American University at Beirut is perhaps the best example. Here, where collections of Western books can be applied directly to the transmission of Western ideas, they reach perhaps their maximum effectiveness.

A third major instrument consists, obviously, of the libraries of indigenous universities and research institutions. The strengthening of their holdings has been the object of many efforts since 1945. At the close of the war, American libraries and related interests united to form the American Book Center for War Devastated Areas, Inc. This agency was responsible for soliciting, collecting, screening, and shipping hundreds of thousands of volumes to aid in restoring the collections of institutions abroad. Though the majority of its shipments were to European institutions, its services to those of Asia were great. Even after the immediate postwar emergency was met, it was obvious that there was need for a continuing agency which could provide a channel for the flow of books from American libraries and similar institutions to those abroad, but on a basis primarily of exchange rather than gift. To meet this need there was created in 1948 the United States Book Exchange, a non-profit corporation physically housed in the Library of Congress, but entirely private in character, representing American libraries and learned societies. It is the function of this agency to receive suitable duplicates and current publications and to exchange them, primarily with institutions abroad (though failing that with other American institutions) for materials desired by American libraries. American institutions are entitled to claim a foreign book for each two or three they deposit, and a reverse ratio applies to foreign institutions. The USBE was initially financed by a grant from the Rockefeller Foundation and is now maintained by a modest handling fee per volume received assessed against American libraries and those foreign libraries able to pay it, by grants from the State Department, and by contracts with various groups for which it may perform services. Approximately 30,000 publications a year, usually specifically requested by title, are now sent abroad on exchange by USBE. Over 300 foreign institutions, including 81 in Asia and Africa, participate actively in these exchanges. In addition, USBE screens, selects recipients for, and ships donations of books for foreign libraries received by or through the State Department and by a number of other organizations. Such shipments, handled in whole or in some part by USBE, still constitute by far the major part of its program in bulk if not in long-range importance, and now run at the rate of some half-million volumes a year.

Many direct exchanges are also carried on by individual American institutions, notably by the Library of Congress and its sister Federal institutions, the Medical Library of the Armed Services and the Department of Agriculture Library. The Library of Congress carries on exchanges with slightly under 7500 institutions of which 1600 are in the area of interest to us. It sends abroad over 100,000 publications a year in addition to the 101 sets of Federal documents supplied foreign institutions on official exchanges—of which 16 sets go to countries in our area.

As noted in the case of the USBE, however, gifts still provide a far larger non-commercial flow of publications abroad than do exchanges. The State Department undertakes such gifts to foreign libraries through two programs— that of the Information Center Service of the International Information Administration and that of the Technical Cooperation Administration, better known as the Point Four Program, with the former handling materials primarily in the fields of history, the social sciences, and current public affairs and the latter scientific and technical publications. In neither program has a great deal been accomplished, in part because the contrast between almost limitless need and very limited resources has discouraged any large-scale effort and in part because the highly specific character of the objectives each of those programs seeks to achieve with a limited budget seems to require a relatively low priority for general presentations of books to foreign libraries.

So far as the Information Center Service is concerned, however, I believe that this very limited emphasis has been a mistake. A position has now been established in that Service devoted solely to cooperation with foreign libraries, and it it hoped to have for the coming year a materially larger budget for this purpose. If so, it is expected that a major part of these sums will be used to aid Eastern university libraries to build up their teaching and research resources in recent history and the social sciences.

The State Department will, in any case, be able to do so in India, as the terms of the wheat loan to that country provide that the first $5,000,000 paid in interest shall be devoted to cultural exchanges between India and the United States. Beginning next year, this arrangement will provide substantial sums for the purchase of books for Indian university and research libraries. It should be noted that this provision is patterned on the similar and highly successful arrangement for applying Finland's war debt payments to cultural exchanges with that country.

Various efforts have been made to channel private gifts to aid the flow of books abroad. You are all familiar with the generous if too frequently misdirected enthusiasm of "book drives." The miscellaneous product of these donations always requires extensive screening, and they generally pass through the USBE. Less spectacular but perhaps more useful have been the efforts of various learned societies and professional groups to provide specialized publications in their respective fields. Both CARE and UNESCO have collected funds for the purchase of current publications for foreign institutions. CARE's program has sent abroad many hundreds of thousands of dollars worth of scientific and technical publications, primarily to Europe. UNESCO's gift coupon scheme, which works rather like its regular book coupon program except that the funds are derived from private donation, has been in operation for only a relatively short time, but offers great promise for Eastern institutions.

Perhaps for the same reason that has limited government enterprise in this field—the discouragement that comes from needs so hopelessly outrunning resources—the great American foundations have done little to contribute to the holdings of Asian university and research libraries.

Finally, I should mention that the principal countries of Western Europe have endeavored to aid Asian libraries along most of the lines described above though on a much smaller scale; and many of the Asian countries themselves have made heroic efforts in terms of their resources to provide the foreign currencies needed to develop their university resources.

Even the most successful efforts to enrich the collections of university and research libraries in this area will be fruitless, however, unless they are accompanied by measures to improve their competence. Here again many programs have been in operation. The United States through its exchange of persons program has sent leaders abroad to teach and to advise in the development of library services. Most of these have been in the field of public library service, to which I shall refer later; but as indicative of the work to be done in university and research librarianship, I may mention the highly successful service of Dr. Lawrence Thompson, Librarian of the University of Kentucky, in his recent mission to Turkey on a State Department grant. Similarly, many leading foreign librarians have been brought to the United States for study. From Asia and the Near East alone there have recently come Dr. Joseph A. Dagher of the Lebanese National and Lebanese University Libraries, Dr. Abdel Moneim Omar of the Egyptian National Library, Dr. S. R. Ranganathan of the University of New Delhi, Dr. B. S. Kesavan of the Indian National Library, and Dr. Gabriel A. Bernado of the University of the Philippines.

UNESCO has been similarly devoted to the development of university and research libraries, and has recently provided technical advisory missions for the library of the Syrian University of Damascus and for all university libraries in Iran, beginning with that of Tehran.

The Technical Cooperation Administration has given limited assistance in the development of research libraries abroad in specific fields of agriculture, public health and the like.

But the strengthening of university and research library services involves something more than enlarging collections and training personnel. It involves also technical apparatus— in the bibliographical sense—and the initiation of bibliographical services. In this field the Library of Congress has played an especially important role among American institutions through the very widespread gift of its cumulative Author Catalog and Subject Catalog, its lists of subject headings, its classification schedules, and other technical tools. The Medical Library of the Armed Services and the Department of Agriculture Library have been similarly generous within their respective fields.

But here again the lead has been taken by UNESCO. In addition to work in other areas, it has sent missions to Ankara to establish a National Bibliographic Center in the Turkish National Library, and to New Delhi to establish a similar center for South Asia. It has established an International Bibliography and Documentation Committee and is preparing a Manual on the Organization of National Bibliographical Centers. It is producing a new edition of the Index Bibliographicus, and its advisory services are always available to research institutions in the less developed countries.

10.

Finally we come to measures intended to aid the Asian and Near Eastern countries in developing the machinery for disseminating among their peoples, through books and libraries, the knowledge and ideas required or adapted from the West.

These fall into two general areas: aid in the development of local school and public library systems, and aid in the development of local book production.

The development of local library systems as instruments for the internal dissemination of knowledge has engaged the intense interest of many Eastern governments. The Philippines, India, Burma and Thailand in particular have enacted legislation or adopted programs that press toward national systems extending throughout the rural areas of their countries. Difficult as the early steps are, without resources of funds and training, one is nevertheless deeply impressed by the vitality of these movements and by the clear realization of many national leaders of the area that libraries are essential instruments of national development.

The United States has endeavored to aid these national movements in several ways, all subject to severe budgetary limitation. The educational missions of the Point Four Program have aided in the development of the school library concept. Through its exchange of persons program the State Department has sent a number of Americans abroad to work in school, public, and extension library development, including Mary Gaver to conduct workshops in Tehran, Louise Galloway to work with the Philippine Department of Education, Budd Gambree to work in Cairo, Ruth Rockwood to teach library science at Chulalonghorn University in Thailand, and Frances Spain to conduct library institutes in that country. Many librarians of United States Information Centers abroad have devoted themselves to aiding local library movements in addition to their regular jobs. Emily Dean in Ankara and Lucille Dudgeon in Cairo have particularly distinguished themselves in this regard. Insofar as it could, the Department of State has tried also to aid local public libraries through gifts, especially in the Philippines; but the fact that the great need is for simple material in indigenous tongues has limited the effectiveness of this approach. Through "expendable libraries" of inexpensive reprints placed in thousands of sets throughout India the State Department has also demonstrated a possible technique for local adaptation.

Here again UNESCO has really taken the lead. The development of effective public librarianship, especially in underdeveloped areas, has been one of its consistent and energetically pursued aims. In addition to publishing a number of helpful aids in this field, it has conducted a seminar on public libraries and adult education at Malmo, Sweden, and one on public librarianship for Latin Americans at Sao Paulo. One is planned for African librarians in Achimota in 1953.

UNESCO and the Government of India opened a jointly supported public library at Delhi in October 1951 which was intended to serve as an experimental and demonstration project not only for India but for all South Asia. This has already proved to be a definite success as a demonstration and training center, and the experiment one hopes will be repeated in other Asian countries.

11.

As Frank M. Gardner, the English librarian serving as a consultant on the Delhi project pointed out in his report on the initial year's operation, the success of any such demonstration project or of any public library system depends upon the availability of an adequate body of vernacular materials suitable for popular library use. And here we run into the most fundamental and stubborn of all our problems: the creation of the books that are needed for the dissemination of Western knowledge and ideas within Eastern cultures. It is also the problem about which we have done least.

UNESCO has applied itself to the development of primers and elementary texts that will serve as tools in literacy programs and at the same time convey rudimentary technical and social material. Missions for this purpose have been sent to Egypt, Iraq, Nigeria, and the Gold Coast in the region of our interest. A fundamental education center which has the development and production of such materials as one of its functions has been established in Mexico, and it is intended to be followed by one in Egypt which will serve all the Arab states. The American Point Four Program less systematically, has helped in the production of somewhat similar materials at a higher educational level.

These outside stimuli have but aided a program which remains, however, almost entirely a national one within each of the Eastern countries. Almost every one of them is making a strenuous effort to produce an adequate flow of textbooks for their schools. In several, such as Pakistan and Thailand and especially the Philippines, American textbook publishers have given material assistance in the techniques of textbook preparation.

As yet, however, few efforts have been made to aid local book publishers. The State Department and the American Book Publishers Council have joined in facilitating the visits of a few foreign publishers to the United States, and it would be desirable for this program to be extended. ECA provided funds for printing equipment for the Burma Translation Society, a government agency devoted to the popular dissemination of Western knowledge.

More ambitious than any of these plans has been the collaboration of the American publishing industry, educational interests, and the State Department in the establishment in 1952 of a non-profit publishing house devoted to foreign language publication. This institution, Franklin Publications, Inc., is operating with a very limited budget which permits only a restricted program of publication in Arabic for the present. But it affords a mechanism through which foundations and similar groups as well as varied governmental agencies can obtain the inexpensive and effective publication and distribution of materials in Asian languages. Franklin Publications, Inc., is, of course, working most closely with publishers and governmental and educational agencies of the countries in which it operates in the endeavor to establish itself as a genuine intellectual bond between the two areas.

12.

I hope that this very summary discussion has at least made clear the awesomeness of the responsibility, the difficulty of the problems, and the complexity of approaches to their solution. I hope, too, that it will have made evident the need of an international educational effort far beyond any we have yet been enabled to make. Never before, I believe, has the weight of the future hung so heavily on the labors of teachers and bookmen. For it will depend very largely on us and on our colleagues abroad whether the commonwealth of knowledge and ideas which lies always before us as the ideal of our professions can be made real and made the basis of a free commonwealth of men—a "one world" in fact.

THE CHALLENGE OF CENSORSHIP*

LUTHER EVANS

Librarian of Congress

1.

The subject of my talk tonight is one that has to be approached with a great deal of calmness. It has to be approached with a real understanding of the issues at stake, with an appreciation of the arguments pro and con for different kinds of solutions of the problem of censorship, particularly censorship in libraries. It seems to me that it is really impossible to understand the problem of censorship without understanding what the roots are of the present hysteria, or near-hysteria, that sometimes develops in this country, particularly at the community level.

It seems to me that the psychological unsettlement in which the American people find themselves today is primarily attributable to one enormous fact, namely, that they have more responsibility in the world than they know how to discharge. Things have gone wrong with our policies and our efforts, and the people do not know what has gone wrong. To some degree they have tried to find someone who is guilty of having misled us. In other words, the people feel guilty that this country does not know fully how to behave in the present-day world and to discharge its responsibilities well. But a people hardly ever is willing to accept guilt for long. Before long the feeling triumphs that the people are not guilty, but rather someone must have tricked them. The American people are thus now engaged in hunting the scoundrels who have kept us at various times from succeeding in some of our international efforts. We fought two world wars, but we have not achieved peace.

The world is worse off than it was before we fought the Second World War. What has gone wrong? Ah, they say, somebody betrayed us at Yalta. What went wrong in China?

*A public lecture given at Florida State University, Tallahassee, February 12, 1953. On July 1, 1953, Mr. Evans became Director General of UNESCO.

Ah, they say, some of those smart little leftist crooks in the State Department hoodwinked General George Marshall—that is the reason we lost China.

Well, the answer that I give is "nonsense." That is not the reason we lost China; and what happened at Yalta is no explanation of the progress the Russians have made in the world against us in the past decade. The explanation lies elsewhere. There are other causes that would have worked if there had been no Yalta; and there are other causes that would have worked to put China in the hands of the Communists, no matter what we did, unless we had been willing to abandon our principle of respect for the national sovereignty of other countries, or had ourselves taken over China by force. That is the only thing that would have kept China out of the hands of the Communists. But the American people will not believe that. They want to find a scapegoat. They are not willing to take the responsibility for deciding what is the kind of a world we live in, and that the remedies for it have got to be something that we have never tried yet. We are not ready to face the fact of the world we are in and we are not ready to face the fact that our own policies are inadequate to deal with that situation. So that what the American people are doing is like jumping up and down on a hot skillet. That, I think, is the fundamental background of this hysteria.

I could find you and quote to you statements of individual leaders in this country who have said at different times that we went too far in certain policies, and then later on that we did not go far enough, or vice versa. I will give you one, just to illustrate this point. Senator Robert Taft said in relation to one of our policies that was hostile to Soviet Russia, that there was not enough evidence to believe that Russia was out to conquer the world, as claimed by President Harry Truman and Secretary Deane Acheson. And on other occasions not much later, he said in substance that the Truman Administration had not yet waked up to the fact that the Russians were trying to conquer the world, and had been hoodwinking the Truman Administration. Now which way would Senator Taft like to have it? It is not both ways, because he was talking about a policy that had been rather constant. When he made the first statement, Senator Tom Connally remarked that he didn't agree and added that down in Texas, when someone shoots at you, you can be pretty sure he is against you. Now, all these statements I have referred to are in the *Congressional Record*.

But I am not going to make a speech here against Senator Taft or for Senator Connally, or against the Republicans, or against the Democrats, because what I am saying could be illustrated from both sides of the party line. Americans know that something is wrong, and hence a movement gets started to root the traitors out of Government; and I have no doubt that there were some disloyal people in the Government. I do not think there were very many in the period since World War II. We found one or two persons who looked very much like Communists in the Library of Congress, much to our surprise. The method of investigation that we used uncovered them. I am convinced that the cases of subversion and disloyalty that have been found in the Government are not sufficient to justify the amount of fear of subversion and disloyalty which has swept the country.

Once this fear became strong, a lot of people decided to get what they could out of it. A lot of people who did not believe that the facts were very bad decided to use them for all they were worth for their own purposes. I suppose you know, although I am not sure Florida is a good place to learn it, that politicians will do almost anything to get elected, and that if they can get elected by feeding the people unreasoning fear, they will do that just as quickly as they will feed the people the truth. And many politicians have found that this fear is something they can exploit in order to get into office, and some of them have been doing it with a vengeance.

2.

Now, one aspect of this fear to which I wish to address myself is this: The doctrine that we must fight the ideas that are our enemies; hence we must fight not only Communism, but all the ideas that are between us and Communism and which look like that they might lead us to Communism. This means particularly Socialism, but also, the argument goes, everything that is "un-American," as though you could not be good unless you were American. And the doctrine goes on to say this stuff is poison and we must keep it from spreading. And how do we keep it from spreading? If it's printed, we get rid of it—if it has not been printed, let's try to stop it from being printed.

That this is one of the techniques used by those who fear ideas is not something that I have just discovered. John Milton wrote about it back in the 17th century: "But the harm that may result hence," that is, from statements of vice, in his terminology, is usually reckoned as being of three kinds. "First, is fear'd the infection that may spread; . . ." The people who would deprive us of freedom of speech, of freedom of the press, sometimes are doing it for this reason which was well recognized in the 17th century. They are afraid the poison will spread. They take the opposite view from what Milton stated, which was as follows: "And though all the windes of doctrin were let loose to play upon the earth, so Truth be in the field, we do injuriously by licencing and prohibiting to misdoubt her strength. Let her and Falsehood grapple; who ever knew Truth put to the wors, in a free and open encounter. Her confuting is the best and surest suppressing." That Thomas Jefferson had read Milton is quite clear from his statement that ". . . truth is great and will prevail if left to herself . . . unless . . . disarmed of her natural weapons, free argument and debate."

Now, there is the critical issue in censorship, and it is the critical issue that is being raised today. The feeding of this movement is I think coming largely from the fear and frustration that I mentioned earlier. This movement was not entirely created by Senator Joseph McCarthy, but it bears his name, and we might as well refer to it as McCarthyism. I have referred to it that way in the Library of Congress *Information Bulletin*, and the matter has been called to Senator McCarthy's attention. He has raised no objection to it.

Now, of course, when Milton and Jefferson and other

great liberal leaders in this field, including John Stuart Mill from whom I wish to quote in a moment, were talking about censorship, they were thinking in most cases of action by government, but not exclusively that in the case of Mill. Jefferson may have been thinking mostly of government, and Milton was definitely trying to knock a weapon out of the hand of government. Fortunately Milton succeeded. A few years after his eloquent appeal was published, in the year before our own Declaration of Independence, the English Parliament withdraw the licensing for the publication of books that was the principal weapon of censorship. And since then, there has been a pretty free press in Britain.

In the case of the McCarthy movement, the principal operational method of censorship is of two kinds. One of them has been there in some measure much earlier, but this movement has strengthened it. And that is national group pressure on the media of communication, to prevent the putting of certain facts and ideas and views in those media of communication. Thus, Jewish groups tried to keep *Oliver Twist,* the movie, from being shown, on the ground that it was derogatory to the Jews. Thus, certain Catholics tried to have the *Miracle* banned as being derogatory to the Catholic Church. I give you these two examples, but there are many many others that could be given. These group pressures are always present to some degree in our society. We cannot get away from them, but we should watch them and make sure that they do not go so far as to interfere with the substantial presentation of varying points of view about great social issues. Some of these movements now are backfiring; the courts have knocked down a statute which censored the *Miracle,* and the Jewish groups lost their battle to keep *Oliver Twist* from being shown in American theaters. I have seen the latter movie and while the person pictured in the movie, as in the book, is Jewish and is a despicable character, it did not make me change my mind about the Jews, it did not make me a Jew hater, it did not lower the Jews in my estimation; it has nothing to do with the American Jews in the first place, and it has nothing to do with the contemporary period. I have not seen the *Miracle,* and hence do not know whether it contains highly objectionable things or not. But we have to tolerate things which are highly objectionable to some of us if we are not to lose our freedom.

It is all right in a democracy that has freedom of the press, freedom of speech, and freedom of religion for people to be objectionable to others. This country would not exist without it. How would we ever have achieved separation of State and Church in this country if people had not said objectionable things about churches, about organized religion? We would not have made that kind of progress, without this freedom that we have.

John Stuart Mill states very well this whole problem that is before us. In his day, a century ago, they were increasing their democracy in England and that was resulting in attacks on the rights of property. It was resulting in attacks along many fronts in the field of social progress, in the field of freedom of working men to organize, and so forth. "The notion," he says, "that a government should choose opinions for the people, and should not suffer any doctrines in politics, morals, law, or religion, but such as it approves, to be printed or publicly professed, may be said to be all together abandoned as a general thesis. It is now well understood that a régime of this sort is fatal to all prosperity, even of an economical kind: that the human mind when prevented by fear of the law or by fear of opinion from exercising its faculties freely on the most important subjects, acquires a general torpidity and imbecility, by which, when they reach a certain point, it is disqualified from making any considerable advances even in the common affairs of life, and which, when greater still, make it gradually lose even its previous attainments. There cannot be a more decisive example than Spain and Portugal, for two centuries after the Reformation. The decline of those countries in national greatness, and even in material civilization, while almost all the other nations of Europe were uninterruptedly advancing, has been ascribed to various causes, but there is one which lies at the foundation of them all: the Holy Inquisition, and the system of mental slavery of which it is the symbol."

"Yet although these truths are very widely recognized, the freedom both of opinion and of discussion is admitted as an axiom in all free countries, this apparent liberality and tolerance has acquired so little of the authority of a principle, that it is always ready to give way to the dread and horror inspired by some particular sort of opinions. Within the last 15 or 20 years,"—I don't know when this was written, but somewhere around 1850—". . . several individuals have suffered imprisonment for the public profession, sometimes in a very temperate manner, of disbelief in religion; and it is probable that both the public and the government, at the first panic which arises on the subject of Chartism or Communism, will fly to similar means for checking the propagation of democratic or anti-property doctrines."

This statement came after 1848, because it was in 1848 that the Communist Manifesto was issued. I hope the students in this University all read the Communist Manifesto. You are not in my opinion well equipped to fight Communism until you know the Communist Manifesto almost by heart. Mill continues: "In this country, however, the effective restraints on mental freedom proceed much less from the law or the government, than from the intolerant temper of the national mind; arising no longer from even as respectable a source as bigotry or fanaticism, but rather from the general habit, both in opinion and conduct, of making adherence to custom the rule of life, and enforcing it, by social penalties, against all persons who, without a party to back them, assert their individual independence."

I think I can tell you that although the number of specific instances that have come to public notice of pressures being put on public libraries, to withdraw or not to have certain books in their collections is not a large number of cases, there probably has been an enormous amount of self discipline on the part of local librarians to keep certain things out of their collection for fear that there would be difficulty if they had them in their collections. Hence I think it probable that a great deal of censorship is practiced on the sly, and it is to make an appeal against that kind of cowardice that I am here this evening. There was one young lady, a young people's and children's librarian, as we call them in our profession, who said: "I do not understand all of this talk about trouble over books you have in your library; we never have any difficulty at all; we just send the list of books we intend to buy to the local post of the Americal Legion, and when they approve it, everything is all right and nothing ever happens."

This reminds me of the story, perhaps apocryphal, of the Chapter of the Daughters of the American Revolution which is reported to have asked the local librarian to remove from the library all books that were derogatory to any of the Founding Fathers of this country. The librarian took the matter seriously and when the DAR Committee came back a year later to see what she had done, they were annoyed to find that she had removed to the attic the writings of George Washington, the writings of Thomas Jefferson, the writings of John Adams, Alexander Hamilton, Samuel Adams, Thomas Paine, and so forth. They asked her why she had removed the very sort of thing they wanted people to read. Her answer was that she had to remove all these books because every one of their authors said something derogatory of one or more of the Founding Fathers.

We had a sharp fight recently about having books in the Boston Public Library that deal favorably with Communism. The Librarian took the position that such material had to be in the Library: How can we fight Communism unless we know the doctrines of Communism? I can add that Senatory McCarthy keeps us very busy at the Library of Congress digging up material on Communism. In a speech I made there after the fight was really won, I said that if the Library were to do what the *Boston Post* and other evil influences suggested, it could not retain the *Boston Post,* because the paper frequently quoted what Stalin said against us or our form of government. It seems to me that here is the logic of the situation: Are you going to learn about the evil? Are you going to let the people learn about it? Or are you going to say that the reading matter is poison and must not be allowed to spread? If it's poison and must not be allowed to spread, then perhaps we ought to prevent Senator McCarthy from telling us what Communism preaches, because we might become infected. Need I say, I do not propose that we should do this?

Here is what John Milton said: "Since therefore the knowledge and survay of vice is in this world so necessary to the constituting of human vertue, and the scanning of error to the confirmation of truth, how can we more safely, and with lesse danger scout into the regions of sin and falsity than by reading all manner of tractats, and hearing all manner of reason? And this is the benefit which may be had of books promiscuously read."

That is his doctrine. If you want to deal with evil, study it. If you want to deal with false arguments, you must read those false arguments. Now, the people who take the other side are not only flying in the face of Americanism in its purest form, they also are undermining democracy, because the doctrine of poison spreading is a doctrine that the people can't be trusted to learn and to judge. If you believe that the American people would succumb to Communist doctrine merely by being exposed to it in books and magazines and newspapers—I am not talking now about what you teach in the schools—then you do not believe the American people have enough sense to govern themselves.

I think, if I may say so, that the doctrine of freedom of the press and freedom of speech is far more basic an American doctrine than is the doctrine that you cannot overthrow the government by force or violence. I think that the idea you should not overthrow the government by force and violence is one of the basic American doctrines, if the conditions of the Declaration of Independence are satisfied, but not if these conditions are not satisfied. I mean that it is not good American doctrine that you can overthrow the government by force and violence in cases where the evils described in the Declaration of Independence are not present. I mean that we can fight with all our might against the overthrow of the government by force and violence today, because today we are being governed democratically. But we want to preserve the doctrine that if the government is not governing according to democracy, that if we should have a tyranny in this country, that if the Communists should seize our government, we would then still have the right of revolution, the right to overthrow the government.

We are preaching that doctrine of the right of revolution to the Czechs and to the other peoples who are under Communist rule. We want them to rise—we are not advocating that they do it at the moment, but we are supporting the doctrine that they have the right to do so. Now, I did not say that the Communist doctrine is more nearly the American doctrine than destruction of freedom of speech. I have said that the Communist doctrine, as applied to America today, is unjustified because our government is democratic. But our own doctrine of the right of revolution might well be used against Communist dictatorship here or somewhere else.

3.

Now, let me talk a little bit about another aspect of the matter. There is a problem here, and what I have said so far is not enough to meet it. People in various communities are raising questions about what is being taught the children in the schools and what is being furnished the people in the libraries. Let us take a look, they say, at the motion pictures put out by the United Nations that are circulating in our community. The people have a right to look into such questions, it seems to me. I insist that if the American Legion wants to look at a United Nations movie, and see whether it is a menace to the country, in their opinion, there can be no objection to their doing it. I have no objection to their doing it even if all they say about it is to point out its faults. I accept the basic doctrine that you can fight falsehood with truth and that you cannot muzzle people just because what they say is false or misguided. Finding truth is not an automatic or certain process and all are entitled to express their views.

An interesting example of how to meet such a situation is afforded by the Peoria case. As a minor participant in this controversy over an attempt by certain local groups to force the withdrawal from the public library of a motion picture on the Universal Declaration of Human Rights put out by the

United Nations, I believe that a very interesting and fruitful procedure for dealing with certain kinds of censorship controversies has been found. What they do in Peoria is provide an opportunity, in the case of a newly acquired film which may raise social issues, for representatives of community groups to preview the film and to make their written comments on it. Such comments as are turned in are put in a folder under the name of the film and are made available to but not foisted upon any prospective borrower of the film. Thus, all the various local judgments can be brought to bear on the question whether a film is true, false, subversive, good, bad, indifferent, of no account, or what. Personally, I have advocated that this be one of the principal techniques that local libraries use in dealing with demands for censorship.

Thus, if the American Legion comes to the library and asks: "have you got Communist books?" I would not say "go away—this is none of your business." I would say "let's sit down and take a look," and then I would show them the list of recommended readings on Communism that the National Headquarters of the American Legion published; and then say "well now, shouldn't these books be here for people to look at? Let's make sure that we have books that answer the Communist books. But shouldn't they be here? Wouldn't you like to be able to read Karl Marx's *Das Capital?*—a most unreadable book—but if anybody wants to read it, shouldn't he be allowed to read it? If he wants to read the Communist Manifesto, shouldn't he be allowed to read it?" And if you sit down and argue with a group like this, you can usually win.

The Peoria post took the fight on the United Nations film which they could not get out of the library, to the State Legion, and the State Legion of Illinois refused to back the doctrine that the film ought to be taken out of the library. So that when you grapple with this problem and don't just stand on your rights, you sometimes make converts, and you persuade people who are good in their intentions but misguided in their methods, and convert their good intentions to a defense of American liberties and the American doctrine.

Another important thing that librarians have done to defend themselves in censorship battles is to have their governing boards develop a statement of acquisitions policy and then when anyone objects to a particular book's being in the library, the members of the board will defend the particular application of the acquisitions' policy and take the librarian off of the hot spot by defending what has been done. But in order to be able to do that you have to have a statement of policy to fall back upon. If you do not have a statement of acquisitions policy, it becomes much more difficult to defend acquisitions actions.

At this point let me state a view of what the role of the librarian is in relation to truth. Some people have claimed that the library's job is to present the truth; I disagree with that. If the librarian has to present the truth, then the librarian has to take responsibility for knowing the truth, and if you are put in the position of having to know the truth on all subjects to all comers, you take refuge in neutrality and sterility, and that is what librarians have done to too great a degree; they have taken hands off of a lot of issues, and stayed away from the literature on a lot of issues because those issues were considered hot.

The safe course, I am convinced, is for the librarian to say "I don't know anything, except one thing: Here are the issues; the pro is presented in this book; and the contra in this book; read them and decide for yourself." And if the librarian takes that point of view, then he can become a specialist in knowing where the materials and the arguments may be found for and against every contention. And he can have the most violent arguments there in the literature, and all he has to say is "well, that is what labor says about capital, and that is what capital says about labor," or whatever it may be; "read it for yourself. You ask where is the truth? Read it for yourself, I don't know the truth."

The Library of Congress, if I may be personal for a moment, has been doing this very thing at a high level of responsible research during the past 10 or a dozen years—mostly during the last five or six years at the high research level on practically all of the issues before Congress. The Library of Congress has been telling the Senator who thinks Chiang Kai-shek is mistaken, what the literature says about Chinese problems, and it has been telling the Senators who think that Chiang Kai-shek is the potential savior of mankind, what the literature says about the Chinese situation. And what the Library gives the Senators is used as debate material on both sides, and we have not yet been caught off base in any serious way. The reason for this is the way that we work. They ask us if something is true, and we reply by saying that the views of competent and responsible people, perhaps rather generously interpreted, are as follows; and then we give a variety of views. We take an inescapable responsibility for knowing the sources, and for identifying the important variant views, as well as delineating the issues. No librarian can escape the same responsibility in some degree. Louis Shores has written a book on reference books. The reference function is one that the librarian cannot escape: The function of knowing the sources, and of knowing what the sources say. If the librarian says "I don't know the answer; I merely know the steps toward the answer and you have to take those yourself," then the librarian is above the battle. He then has a justification of having Communist books, because he cannot present two sides of the question without occasionally bringing out the Communist side.

Let's get rid of unreasoning fears. The Communists cannot hurt us much in this country. They can hurt us elsewhere in the world, and they are hurting us elsewhere greviously. And one reason they are hurting us greviously is that we do not always practice what we preach. One reason why the two-thirds of the world which is colored, has questions about white America, is because we preach equality of men and do not fully practice it. We preach freedom of the press, and they see people driven off of the radio and television because someone said they were Red without proving it. Here lies a great danger to our future, to our national security, because we will not win the cold war with Russia, and if the hot war comes, we will not win it unless some of these other peoples who now have great skepticism about us, really join on our side. And every time we drive a commentator off the radio on suspicion, every time we drive a diplomat out of the State Department just because he reported honestly to the State Department that the State Department policies were wrong, we are going to lose votes in those foreign countries. And we have got to have the votes of those foreign countries. We have to have them every day in the United Nations in order for our basic foreign policies to triumph. And I guarantee to you from my experience of travel around the world, and in dealing with diplomats from many countries, in many conferences of UNESCO and in other conferences, that we lose more by the violation of our own basic principles than one can possibly imagine from the ordinary evidence presented to us in this country. You have to go abroad to see it.

The most favorable propaganda is the news that you have as a nation lived up to a great principle. Let me tell you a story that will serve to illustrate this point. One of our great Air Force generals asked why it was that during the recent war Americans who fell over islands in the South Pacific, were hidden by the natives and nearly all of them kept out of the hands of the Japanese who were in occupation of those islands. The reply he received from the natives themselves was that they risked their lives for United States airmen because the United States gave the Philippines their freedom. That was the only answer they had.

I believe that today there is in much of the world unjustified suspicion of our motives, and too much blame put on us. I get angry sometimes when I see how our motives are misinterpreted, but the point which I wish to make is that there is enough reality to the belief that we do not fully live up to our professed ideals to keep suspicion alive, and to make harder our defense of peace and freedom.

4.

I am going to end by reading you a little statement I wrote almost a year ago:

A curious poisoning of the historic spirit of America is taking place at the present time. Were I a psychiatrist I would attempt to diagnose this mental ill of our country which has done great damage to the American spirit at home and to the American reputation abroad, and which, at present reading, seems to threaten much greater damage. In a country which has been one of the few homes in the past two centuries of the spirit of freedom of the press and many other great freedoms, there is abroad in the land today a strong and ugly (and I fear growing) movement for the destruction of certain of these freedoms. Naturally, the effort to destroy the freedom of speech and of the press is made in the name of these and other freedoms themselves. For instance, the effort to destroy the freedom of the public to read in the Peoria Public Library is made in the name of an effort to prevent the United Nations' proposed Covenant on Human Rights from destroying the U. S. Bill of Rights.

Thus we have a situation where the shrillest and most fear-ridden defenders of the Bill of Rights are themselves making specious arguments for the abridgement in spirit of the Bill of Rights itself. Surely this is an attitude of mind which calls for the attention of the best psychiatrists. There must be some deep-seated illness of the spirit, some boundless frustration or sense of guilt which causes Americans to do some of the things they are doing today.

The American public library is one of the great bulwarks of liberty and democracy in this great land. It must remain a place where citizens can go to learn what is to be said for and against all of the proposals made on the great public issues of the day, issues which they either must face or must forfeit the claim to being good citizens. The drawing of lines against the study of this or that proposal, on the ground that it would poison the minds of the people, is abhorrent to the spirit on which this country is founded. Such a setting up of forbidden zones of thought must be fought to the death.

It is not a theoretical danger, this danger against which I am speaking. It is a very real danger and it has caused many librarians throughout this land to chisel a bit on the doctrines by which they have lived in the past. The amount of that chiseling can never be known, because so much of the evidence is locked in the inner consciousness of frightened librarians. This book, that book, this pamphlet, that pamphlet, this motion-picture, that motion-picture is excluded from the selection process because it is feared that some group in the community suffering from this virus, suffering from this illness of the American spirit, may be ready to pounce upon the librarian for choosing it. This poison must be counteracted promptly by brave people, and must be defeated. The complete antidote to the poison is to refuse to yield one inch of the hard-won earth of freedom. Americans must be brought to the realization that this country stands at an historic turning point in the development of world civilization, and that the responsibilities which have been thrust upon us by virtue of our size, our wealth, our efficiency, our adaptability and our moral greatness will lead us, on many occasions, into positions of great difficulty where courage, where stability of direction, where consistency of purpose are absolute requirements, and where we must not yield to the temptation of turning on our own principles and devouring them because we have met with difficulties or been exposed to a confusion of counsel.

The experts in vituperation, the sadists of freedom, are abroad in the land, and they are having a hey-day of it. We must learn not to fear them. We must show them up for what they really are. They are really cowards who are unwilling to live the American dream.

THE CHALLENGE OF MICROPHOTOGRAPHY*

FREMONT RIDER

Librarian, Wesleyan University

1.

If I were to give this paper a text it would perhaps be this paragraph from an early article of mine:

> We may repeat that the library is "the heart of the college," but are we acutely anxious that our assent shall be more than lip service? Do we have a really compelling conviction that on the richness of the blood stream of books constantly flowing through its heart the vitality of every college depends? Are we, as educational pathologists, continually on the alert that our liberties shall not be attacked by that insidiously fatal disease, bibliographical pernicious anemia? Do we profoundly realize that our recitation systems, our examinations, our honors work are, when all is said and done, only devices by means of which we incite students to extract knowledge for themselves from books?

Why do I quote this as a text? Would I suggest that there are any educators who do not know that books play a vital part in the educational process? Not exactly. The point is not do they know; but how profoundly do they know. I suggested this morning that there may be even some librarians who are not completely conscious of the significance which books have in the world that we live in. And I raise this point again at the start tonight because it is correlary to the theme I have been asked to discuss with you. I want continually to remind you that books, the books themselves, are the one thing that is supremely important. It is the immediate accessibility of the texts that they desire that is, to the vast majority of scholars, the only *sine qua non* of library service. There is no possible substitutional service, no amount of bibliographical accessorial machinery, that can for a moment take the place of the books themselves.

I am going to discuss with you tonight a library problem to the possible solution of which I have, during the last ten years, given a great deal of thought. This thought has crystallized in two books and many professional papers, and in dis-

---

* A public lecture given at Florida State University, Tallahassee, February 26, 1953. Mr. Rider is the inventor of the microcard.

cussions before dozens of audiences. The problem in question is not a theoretical one or a philosophical one; it is, instead, an intensely practical one. As a matter of fact it seems to me at once the most puzzling, and also by far the most important of all the problems today facing librarians and educators. It is this: what are we going to do to cope with the tidal wave of printed materials pouring into our research libraries—yearly, weekly, *hourly*—at a rate which threatens, and threatens increasingly, to overwhelm us?

What is a research library anyway? I once defined it as "a collection of all sorts of book, periodical and manuscript materials, assembled together, not for sustained, or for pleasurable, reading—but for the purposes of scholarly investigation." And I added: "Research libraries are the stored-up knowledge of the race, warehouses of fact and surmise, the raw material from which our humanists and scientists are going to develop for us new facts and fresh surmises." The materials to be found in a research library are literally the building blocks of civilization; and, because they are just that, the storage function of a research library—the sheer holding of the records of the race, not perhaps for any immediate use, but for some possible, but possibly very remote, future use—is one of the extremely important, but not very well understood, reasons for its existence.

Research materials share in common three characteristics. One of the most significant of these characteristics is a somewhat paradoxical one: they are seldom read. Usually the research worker makes only a "reference" use of his books. He wants to verify a date, to find a chemical formula, to check the terms of an equation, to note the phraseology used in a legal decision, to review a psychological reaction, to obtain a map, to look at an anatomical drawing.

The second characteristic common to all research materials is that they are little used. The law of averages would of itself make this true. If a given university has a million volumes and ten thousand students, and if nine thousand of its students are of undergraduate grade, and one thousand of them are at the graduate level, it will be found that, of the books in its libraries, 100,000 are servicing, and are servicing entirely adequately, its undergraduate student body, while its remaining 900,000 volumes are being held solely, or almost solely, for graduate and faculty use. These figures, you will note, work out to a hundred-to-one ratio; that is, on the average, its undergraduate books are getting a hundred times as much use as its research books.

When we examine sample bits of research material we see at once why the use of any one bit is likely to occur at widely separated intervals. Research workers are always working on intellectual frontiers. They are continually pushing out keen observation, shrewd guess, and brilliant deduction in that black unknown country of the mind that surrounds on every side the tiny half-lit spot that we call "knowledge." Our book and periodical research materials are the concrete embodiment of these intellectual frontiers. Each year new research pushes each frontier out farther. But, as every frontier gets stretched thus thinner and thinner, it is obvious that the use made of each segment of the library's materials tends to get steadily less. Indeed, one can go so far as to say that, if something that was previously considered to be research material comes to be frequently used, that very frequency of use shows that it has ceased to be research material!

The third characteristic common to all research materials is that they are used—and that they can be used—only by persons who have gained a certain level of intellectual competency, that is by those whom, for want of a better word, we call "scholars." Furthermore, each scholar is completely competent only in the handling of his own particular segment of the frontier. Few scholars can so much as understand the meaning of the terms used in fields quite outside their own. (Only the librarian—alas!—is assumed to have a sort of intellectual omniscience!)

All of these three characteristics—relatively short use, relatively infrequent use, and relatively high specialization in use—should be constantly kept in mind in every consideration of the problem of research library growth. They are all obvious characteristics; but, just because they are obvious, we have tended not to keep them in mind; and this tendency has, in the past, frequently, and quite unnecessarily, complicated our analyses of the problem and led us to false conclusions regarding its solution.

2.

Research library growth is in no sense a newly discovered fact. Librarians have been well aware for a great many years that all research libraries continually grow larger, and do so both steadily and rapidly. And they have been also well aware that this growth was necessary, in other words that there exists a direct relationship between the educational effectiveness of a college or university and the rate of the growth of its library, a relationship so close and so consistent that it cannot be fortuitous. We found, in studying our statistics, that if, in any given case, there appeared to be a variation from the growth norm that there was always some special explanation for the variation. If, down through the years, the growth of a given library fell below normal we always, on investigation, found that this was a period when its university was slipping educationally. If, on the other hand, we found a library spurting ahead of the normal rate, we always found, on checking further, that that library's university was simultaneously spurting ahead scholastically.

In fact all the records of library growth show clearly that we can premise this as axiomatic: unless a university is willing to fall behind, unless it is willing *not* to hold its relative place in the national educational picture, it must increase the size of its library at a relatively very rapid rate. It does not matter whether we choose to argue that a strong university insists upon having a strong library, or that a strong library develops a strong university: the clearly emergent fact is that the two situations always accompany each other. In other words, there is involved a very real growth norm.

What is it? I just said that we have always known that all research libraries were growing larger rapidly. But, in the past, this realization of growth was a generalized one. In my book *The Scholar and the Future of the Research Library*

I collected, and correlated, a considerable mass of statistical evidence that seemed to show that this growth norm, this curve of research library growth, was both an amazingly uniform one and also actually an exponential one. It appeared that all research libraries—men's colleges, women's colleges, old universities, new universities (it does not matter materially what category one chooses) *all* of them—are doubling in size about every sixteen years. Nor is this doubling process in any sense a recent phenomenon. *The Scholar* showed that, as far back as we can gather evidence, this rate of growth has been a persistent one.

But, if such an exponential curve as this exists, what are its implications? To what sort of a situation does a doubling in size every sixteen years inevitably lead? I presented the answer to this question with somewhat dramatic concreteness in a paper which I read at the University of Chicago back in the summer of 1940. In this paper I took the Yale University Library as my example, choosing it simply because for it there were two hundred years of statistics available.

Let me summarize them. In the early part of the eighteenth century, the Yale library possessed about 1,000 volumes. If it had continued from this start to double in size every sixteen years, it should, in 1938 have had 2,600,000 volumes. In 1938 it actually did have 2,748,000 volumes, which is obviously an exceedingly close correspondence to the normal growth curve. Not only was there this correspondence between the beginning and the end of Yale's record but all of its intervening statistics were also in close correspondence. In 1849, for example, the Yale Library should, according to formula, have had 60,000 volumes. It actually had 50,481.

Now, in physical terms, what do 2,748,000 volumes mean? Well, they mean, for one thing, eighty miles of shelving to store them. They mean, for another, card catalogs occupying somewhere around ten thousand drawers. They mean, for still another, that to service itself in 1938 the Yale library required a staff of over two hundred persons, of whom half were catalogers (or other persons engaged in preparational processes). But, when they are translated into mundane terms of this sort, the future implications of an exponential curve can become outright alarming. Yale's do. Suppose we project the graph of the growth of the Yale Library a century ahead. Of course, it may be objected that it is absurd to attempt to forecast any library's growth a century ahead. Why? The Yale Library is already considerably over two centuries old; Harvard's is three. Why not then add a century more? Particularly when we have found that, just so far as figures for Yale are available, it has not, in even a single decade in its long history, deviated substantially from the normal doubling-every-sixteen-years rate of growth.

But, if the Yale Library does continue to grow at this rate, it will, in 2038, have approximately 200,000,000 volumes, which will occupy over 6,000 miles of shelves. Its card catalog file—if it then has a card catalog file—will consist of nearly three-quarters of a million catalog drawers, which will of themselves occupy not less than eight acres of floor space. New materials will be coming in to it at the rate of 12,000,000 volumes a year; and the cataloging of each year's new acquisitions will require a cataloging staff of over six thousand persons. These figures sound astronomical. They are. But are they any more astronomical than the Yale figures for 1938 would have sounded to the Yale Librarian of 1738?

Of course, my purpose in quoting them here is to fortify my statement that this problem of research library growth is, by all odds, the most serious one that librarians and educators face today. When a library is going from 100,000 volumes to 200,000, or from 200,000 to 400,000, we can somehow plan for its growth; but, when it is soaring upward from 4,000,000 to 8,000,000, or from 8,000,000 to 16,000,000, it is clear that an entirely new sort of planning is called for. Mere palliatives in library technology are going to be utterly ineffective: we now face a situation with which no minor economies in method, no cautious emendations of policy, can possibly cope. We absolutely *must* analyze our whole research library problem from entirely fresh viewpoints, and must endeavor to find, in some entirely different direction, a sweepingly new solution for it.

Nor, I commented in *The Scholar*, can the library and the

educational world much longer delay making this new sort of analysis. Doubling-every-sixteen-years has, as a rate of growth, continued with us now for three centuries, and so far we have been able to cope with it. But, the time is bound to come, sooner or later, when repeated doubling becomes a profoundly disconcerting business. To many librarians this time has either already come or is threateningly imminent.

3.

So much for the problem. What *are* we going to do about it? There have, in the past, been a number of so-called solutions. Most of you are familiar with them: they bear such appelations as "weeding out," "warehouse libraries," "regional storage," "division of subject fields," "inter-library loans," etc., etc. But, when one analyzes all of these "solutions," one finds that they all attempt to solve the problem of growth, so far as any given library is concerned, simply by stopping (in certain directions) the growth of that particular library. Instead of that library's continuing to provide its scholars with the materials that they want, it is proposed that they get a portion at least of the materials they want from somewhere else. If the "warehouse" solution is the one proposed the "somewhere else" is at least to be near by, and so fairly easily reached. If the "regional storage" solution is the one proposed the "somewhere else" is to be scores, or perhaps hundreds, of miles away; but at least we know where it is to be. In the case of the "weeding out" and "division of subject fields" solutions it is usually not at all clear where the "somewhere else" is to be, or even that there is to be any "somewhere else" at all.

It is obvious, if we thus analyze them, that all these so-called solutions are really confessions of avoidance, not solutions. If a research library stops growing in any direction, or directions, it simply ceases to be able to give, in those directions, the service which it was set up to give. Perhaps it should not have attempted to give service in those directions. It may be true that in certain fields, for certain purposes, and for certain types of scholarly need, inter-library loans from "somewhere else" can give the library's own clientele an adequate service. But it must be fully realized that these discontinuances of local service are substitutions for library growth, not methods of making growth continuance possible.

And the essential question is: are they adequate substitutions? On one point all scholars seem to be astonishingly unanimous. They have one desire which, to the layman, sometimes seems to be a quite unreasonable one. They want the texts of their research materials available to them, not a thousand miles away in New York or Chicago or California, but under their own finger tips in Florida, or wherever else it may be that they are working. On all other points they will compromise. If you will only give them in their own library the book they want they are entirely willing to accept that book in almost any physical form. Such exteriosa as binding and cataloging they also deem relatively unimportant. What they want is their *texts;* but these texts they want immediately at hand.

The very fact that this scholarly demand for the immediate availability of the text is so nearly a unanimous one should make us librarians realize that there must be a real reason behind it. There is a reason, and it stems from the fact that research use is very often an *unanticipated* use. A chemist, desiring in the middle of an experiment to check up on some previous report of the reaction which he expected to get but is not getting, isn't going to be helped at all by your offer to borrow from Columbia the text of that report. An astronomer, seeing an unexpected patch of light on one of last night's plates, and wanting to make another plate tonight, isn't going to be satisfied to wait a week for a journal article that refers to a similar light patch. An English professor, hurrying to get a lot of page proofs back to his publisher, and desiring to verify a quotation, isn't going to think that your proposal to secure the book he wants on inter-library loan from Stanford is, in his case, a completely satisfactory library service. Nor does it seem to any of these men at all pertinent that the item that each wants so urgently will probably not be asked for again by anyone for another ten years. And, as a matter of fact, it isn't pertinent.

The reason why library growth is a problem is, of course, that it entails expenditure. These expenditures fall into four main categories—acquisition, cataloging, binding and storage. And of these the greatest is storage. Cataloging cost comes second simply because every research library secures a large proportion of its materials free of purchase cost. Since every item a library acquires involves at least three of these four costs—and many items all four—and since all four costs are substantial ones, it is obvious that no solution of the growth problem is going to be an adequate one unless it meets squarely all four of these costs, and adds to them no significant new ones. Is there any such a solution?

And—to be immediately more specific—is microtext it?

4.

It was about fifty years ago that the first form of microtext—microfilm—entered the library picture. It was at once hailed as the answer to several of the library's cost problems; and, as a matter of fact, it did go a very long way indeed in the right direction. It reduced acquisition cost by a half or more; it eliminated binding cost entirely; it reduced storage costs by at least 75%. About cataloging cost it is true, it did nothing; and also, like all other forms of microtext, it introduced a new cost (for reading machines), and interposed a new technique (reading with these machines) which was unpopular with some would-be users. Notwithstanding these two drawbacks microfilm grew steadily in library use. But, though steady, this growth was an extremely slow one: when *The Scholar* appeared eight years ago less than one-thousanth of one percent of all research library materials were available for purchase in microfilm form.

Yet, despite the infinitesmal dent which microfilm had made in library technology, I came more and more to feel, as I mulled over the problem which *The Scholar* presented, that in some form of microtext there lay the way out—and the only way out—of the impasse into which library growth was driving us. And Microcards, as they developed in my mind, were simply an attempt to devise a better form of microtext than microfilm had been, to change it in ways that seemed to make it more directly responsive to the practical needs of the library.

How "more responsive?"

Well, first of all, Microcards are a microtext printed on paper, and sensitized photographic paper is much cheaper than sensitized photographic film. As for binding, Microcards, like microfilm, eliminate it entirely as a cost. And on storage they save from 92% to 96%, where microfilm saves from 75% to 90%. Finally, because Microcards are provided with a complete, and completely standardized, catalog entry, they save their purchasers from 80% to 100% on cataloging cost.

But Microcards are also "more responsive" than microfilm in their physical form. Being flat and tough they withstand handling abuse better than reels of film do; being of standard library catalog card size, they are more quickly taken in and out of storage, and more easily inserted in, and taken out of, reading machines. Also they are more easily carried in the pocket and sent through the mails.

But this comparison by no means implies that I believe that microfilm is entirely out-moded or that I think that Microcards should, or will, wholly take its place. Quite the contrary. As a matter of fact, for the last two years most of my speaking and writing has been devoted to furthering the idea that a correlation of all of the various forms of microtext into one integrated whole is both possible, and from a library standpoint extremely desirable.

Many librarians feel, however, that microfilm in reel form *is* outmoded: simply because it is unhandy to use, unnecessarily bulky to store, and difficult to file. There is a good deal of anticipation that very soon we are going to come to flat sheet film. For the sake of integration I naturally hope that, when it comes, it will be a sheet film in the international standard catalog card size, so that it can be inter-cataloged with, and interfiled with, Microcards. In Europe, as most of you know, reel microfilm has even now almost gone out of use: Sheet film—"microfiche" as the French call it—of either the standard catalog card size, or of some size very close to it, is there coming into increasing use.

The word I used above was "correlation." "Correlation" assumes that there is a definite place for sheet microfilm in the over-all microtext picture. There is such a place, and it is a perfectly logical, and extremely important, place. Microfilm is indicated—as a physician put it—in all of those very numerous situations (local newspapers are just one example out of many) in which only one copy (or perhaps two or three copies) of a given text is desired. For Microcards, as Miles Price of the Columbia Law Library once succinctly put it, are primarily a method of *publishing,* whereas microfilm is primarily a method of *copying.* His statement simply reflects the fact that microfilm can be economically produced in a one-copy edition whereas Microcards cannot be. The various Microcard publishers never print less than fifteen copies of any title they Microcard: and they prefer to print not less than twenty-five copies. Why? Because it's only when Microcards are produced in quantities that their economy becomes realizable. In a one-copy edition they cost much more than microfilm. (The cost of their cataloging would, by itself, make this last statement true.)

It should be interjected at this point, for very similar reasons, there is also a perfectly logical place for Mr. Boni's "microprint" process, and that it also is a very important place indeed. This place is where the editions desired run to over one hundred copies and do not involve photographic or other very "fine" copy. For the reproduction process which Mr. Boni has ingeniously developed is one that does not require a sensitized paper base. This means that, once initial reproductive costs are covered, duplicative costs are *very* low.

Speaking as a librarian, I am hopeful that he too will eventually decide to provide for his cards the same sort of complete, and completely standardized, catalog entry that Microcards have, and to adopt for them also the international standard catalog card size of card. If he did this his cards would also be interfilable with the other microtext forms in a single file and we would then have that integrated synthesis of all microtext which, from the library standpoint, is so obviously desirable. Not only would each form of text have a field for which it would be particularly suited; but each field would offer substantially equal volumes of possible work.

Where, generally speaking, does microtext development stand today? Obviously it still has not made any really substantial impress upon research library acquisition, for no significant percentage of research materials is as yet available in all of the microtext forms put together. Why not? It this picture likely to change? When? How do Microcards stand at present as compared with microfilm? And finally, what can librarians do to make the microtextual revolution that seems to me ultimately inevitable come about more rapidly?

Let me try to give very brief, and I hope unbiased, answers to these and a few other questions. I emphasize "unbiased" because I am trying to speak this evening, not as the inventor of Microcards, but as a librarian.

5.

Microcards were first mentioned in print eight years ago: they first became available for library purchase five years ago. I said then that it would be ten years before anything like a general acceptance of them by libraries could be expected. Very real progress towards this end has been made. In these five years nearly a thousand American libraries have equipped themselves with Microcard reading machines. In each year of the last five the production of Microcards has approximately doubled. As we have already seen, this business of repeated doubling doesn't make much impression when it starts; but it becomes, almost suddenly, a portentous phenomena. If Microcard production should continue at its present rate it looks as though the "portentous" stage of it might be reached in another two or three years.

Is Microcard production for libraries now ahead of microfilm production for libraries? No. Nowhere near this point. But, one has to repeat, microfilm has had fifty years in which to reach its present volume, Microcards only five. We must also remember that each form of microtext helps each other form. The advent of Microcards has actually helped, not hindered, microfilm development. It is also obvious that research library growth on the one hand, and the pressures of inflation on the other hand, have now reached a point where they are absolutely forcing librarians and educational administrators to see what microtext can do to effect relief for them.

Finally, we must remember that, professionally speaking, librarians are a conservative folk. They look before they leap; and it is eminently proper that they should do so. This may be one reason why a large proportion of Microcard production so far has been developed, not at the behest of libraries, but for such government agencies as the Department of Defense, the Atomic Energy Commission, the Weather Bureau, the U. S. Supreme Court, etc., etc. For these and other similar bodies the Microcard Corporation is at present making thousands of cards every week. It is also true that, of library sales, the larger part so far have been to special libraries (i.e. to commercial research libraries) rather than to college and university libraries. These special libraries may have had graver lacks of basic material; or they may have had more money to spend; or they may have patrons, who, as a class, are a little more ready to accept without demur new bibliological methods.

Can librarians do anything to hasten microtextual development? Obviously they can do a very great deal. How? First by suggesting materials for microtextual reprinting, and second, by buying these materials when they have been printed.

What materials? Microtext has before it three main fields of opportunity. First, to make available to libraries out-of-print materials that are in such short supply that copies of them in book form are either not available at all or have acquired adventitiously high speculative values. Second, to provide a method for the reprinting of very cheap out-of-print materials, materials so cheap that no second-hand bookseller can afford to stock and catalog them, materials, that is, that are being microtexted to save not purchase cost, but storage cost. And, finally—and this third field is, I believe, going to prove increasingly important—microtext provides a method for the original publication of new materials (dissertations as one example) for which purchase demand is too small to justify any sort of book form publication.

This last statement leads directly to another one. Every form of microtext is of itself almost absurdly cheap. And, so long as any form of microtext is bought in a fairly large unit, it is possible for the purchaser to realize fully the benefits of its production economy. But, when an order is given for a single Microcard, for example, the bookkeeping and other handling costs on the order are relatively so large that they wipe out all the economy effected in the card's manufacture. A one-card book or pamphlet, in Microcard form, issued in a hundred copy edition, costs, to manufacture, less than eleven cents. But to fill an order for one copy of such a card, including the getting of it out of stock, its packing and addressing, its billing and collecting, together with its share of general publicational overhead, runs up a total order-handling cost of about thirty-two cents, i.e., a cost three times as large as the cost of the Microcard itself. So all buyers of microtext should, just so far as possible, order it in as large units as possible.

Also they should stimulate the printing of as large initial editions as possible by placing their orders in advance of printing: because the larger the edition the cheaper the unit cost of the item—and by a very wide differential. This is true, to a varying degree, of every sort of microtext.

In general every sort of microtext can cut total library costs on a given book or periodical title from seventy per cent to ninety per cent. And, obviously, this is a very large saving indeed. That is why it seems to me that microtext offers the only way by which we can continue to make available in our own libraries the materials our research workers want us to have for them in them. The more cooperation microtext receives from libraries the more microtext titles there will be available to them, and the faster they will become available. And the greater the amount of correlation we are able to achieve between the various forms of microtext, the lower will be all library costs in buying, housing and using it.

LIBRARIANSHIP AND THE SCIENCES*

CHARLES HARVEY BROWN

Librarian Emeritus, Iowa State College

1.

(APOLOGIA)

Soon after I became librarian of Iowa State College, which is a scientific and technical institution, a scientist, who had just been transferred from the research department of an industrial corporation, visited my office. He asked what seemed to be a simple question, which after 25 years of study I am still unable to answer. He inquired why university libraries did not give the same type of service to a scientist as was given by many libraries of large industrial corporations. I asked him to specify and he listed the following points:

1. Almost immediate availability of all publications needed for his research.

2. Compilation of lists of articles appearing in current journals concerning the specific project on which he was working.

3. Compilation of a bibliography of articles in earlier literature on the project.

4. Assistance in the translation of titles of articles in foreign languages and in the preparation of abstracts of these articles.

I made the rather obvious, but unsatisfactory, reply that sufficient funds were not available for such services. The services of research scientists are extremely valuable and any aid that librarians can give to save their time and to speed up their research should be forthcoming. If increased funds are necessary for adequate bibliographical services to research workers, then such funds should be made available as soon as the needs are clearly presented.

This ideal of service as outlined by my visitor, if it is to be attained, would require a complete revolution of our conception of library service to scientists. It would necessitate changes in types of buildings, acquisition policies, outlook of

*A public lecture given at Florida State University, Tallahassee, March 4, 1953.

library administrators, qualifications of staff members, and even in the curricula and methodology used in library schools, but it would result in a standard of services to scientists not now known, understood or even contemplated.

This paper considers some of the changes necessary in library organization, preparation for librarianship, and in library policies if we are to give to research scientists the bibliographical services they have a right to expect.

2.

This has been called an age of Science. Few, if any of us realize the full implications of this rather trite statement, both for the present and the future. The connotations and implications of scientific discoveries have been lost in a maze of highly specialized researches, important as they are. The scientific changes have brought about during the last fifty years what might be termed social and industrial revolutions.[1] Fortunately, many books which will keep the layman informed of recent scientific developments are appearing. An understanding of the sciences, even if superficial, seems necessary for every librarian, since he may be called upon not only to assist research scientists, but also to give information to the many laymen concerned with scientific advances as well as to scholars in many fields of the humanities who are affected by recent scientific discoveries.

It is, of course, important that librarians understand the needs and points of view of those who use libraries. Unfortunately, this understanding does not exist in all cases and especially in the librarians' relations to the scientists whom they endeavor to serve. The lack of mutual understanding between librarians and scientists can be traced to many causes, some of which can be easily remedied. Few, if any, studies are available which indicate the difficulties scientists have in the use of large university libraries. The case studies listed in this paper are not sufficient in themselves for definite conclusions, but would seem to justify further investigation.

[1] Archibald and Nan S. Clow, "Introduction," *The Chemical Revolution* (London, 1950), pp. xi-xiv.

This paper does not presume to be the result of research studies. It is rather an attempt to state certain beliefs based on forty years of experience in several scientific and technical libraries and on contacts with many scientists in the United States and abroad. The writer is of the opinion that the very tentative inferences presented in this paper can and should be tested by scientific experimentation. The thesis which I should like to defend, subject to future research, is based on the following assumptions:

1. That there is a lack of understanding between librarians and scientists, which has been caused by an inadequate flow of communications between librarians and the scientists who use, or should use, our libraries.

2. That this lack of easy communications has resulted in obstacles in the activities of both scientists and librarians and a lessening of the services both groups should render to society.

3. That the causes for the present lack of mutual understanding can be remedied.

4. That librarianship can profit by a greater application of the scientific method to the functioning of libraries and to the instruction given in library schools.

These four assumptions I should like to consider.

3.

For many librarians the points of view and the requirements of the scientists are difficult to understand and appreciate. Even the nomenclature used by the scientists is a block to communications and a hindrance to the services libraries should render. Some of these difficulties result from four factors:

1. Scarcity of librarians who have majored in the sciences.

2. Lack of emphasis on the sciences in library schools.

3. Lack of communications between the scientists in large universities and librarians.

4. Lack of knowledge by librarians of the scientific method and its applications to librarianship.

In spite of the great development in the sciences in the last fifty years and the wide interest in scientific progress, comparatively few students who enter librarianship have majored in science.[2] There are admittedly some reasons for this deficiency. Students who have ranked high in their scientific courses can obtain much higher salaries by entering industry immediately upon graduation from college. Teachers of science in general are naturally reluctant to encourage their good students to enter librarianship. Furthermore, there is an unfortunate impression that librarianship is chiefly a profession for women and that men who enter the profession are of a retiring nature and do not possess the characteristics of leadership and aggressiveness.

Beginning librarians who do not have any considerable knowledge of science are not apt to increase their knowledge by working in the larger university libraries. These libraries are oriented toward the humanities. The positions of head librarians and heads of departments in our larger university libraries are almost always filled by those who have had their undergraduate training in the humanities. Therefore, the administration of these libraries is determined more by an approach to the humanities than to the sciences. Indeed, some university libraries have been found in which every professional member of the library staff had majored in the humanities.

Library schools, until the last few years, have given little attention to the bibliography and literature of the sciences. Reference courses in many library schools are to a large extent limited to the humanities and the social sciences. In some library schools no member of the faculty has had any considerable background, either through education or experience, in the sciences. Indeed the faculties of all of our library schools are strongly oriented toward the humanities. These conditions are slowly improving. Courses on the bibliography and the literature of the sciences have been introduced into some library schools during recent years, although not in all. Columbia, in the late thirties, may have been the first to introduce such courses, although they were not offered every year. The results of this lack of emphasis in library schools will be illustrated later.

[2]Alice I. Bryan, *The Public Librarian* (New York, 1952), p. 442.

4.

In most of our larger universities, scientific libraries are located in departments apart from the central library. These departmental libraries are not usually closely related to the central libraries. Books and periodicals are selected, and sometimes ordered, by the department concerned without reference to the central library or to other departmental libraries which might be concerned. There are few contacts between the scientists in various departments of the university and the librarians in the central library. Assistants in the central library have little or no connection with scientific books and periodicals and, more important, with the scientists who use such publications. As a result, librarians assigned to duty in the central library of a university are not familiar with the literature of science, nor do they have an opportunity to increase their knowledge by conversations with graduate students and faculty members in the scientific fields. There are even more serious difficulties caused by a highly developed system of inclusive departmental libraries which will be considered later.

5.

Specialists in various branches of the humanities and the sciences do not agree on the definitions of the two terms, science and scientific method. Each discipline prefers definitions which it would like to have applied specifically to studies in its own area. We have terms such as the "science of language," "social science," "science of education," "library science," etc. The definitions used in this paper are generally accepted by specialists in the physical and biological sciences but would be criticized as too exacting by those in other fields. On the other hand, a certain amount of meticulous care is necessary if sound conclusions are to be reached. The failure of research is too often caused by unjustified assumptions and illogical reasoning. One definition in *Webster's Dictionary* defines science as "A branch of study concerned with observation and classification of facts, especially with the establishment of verifiable general laws, chiefly by induction and hypotheses."[3] This definition stresses verifiable knowledge. The scientific method, therefore, requires the collection of factual data which can be verified by other competent research workers. Any general law, principle or conclusion should be thoroughly tested by deductive logic. It will be noted that if the principle of deductive logic had been applied in the cases which will be cited later, the errors would not have occurred.

The collection of factual data is not sufficient in itself. What logical conclusions can be drawn from the data collected? Euclid's famous theorems have stood unchallenged for 2,000 years in so far as finite space is concerned if his postulates, stated as axioms or implied, are accepted. His proofs still remain as models of logical thinking. We are not so fortunate in many of our present day studies. Too often they are based either on erroneous assumptions or illogical conclusions or both. One, not uncommon error, is illustrated by the following syllogism, which is greatly simplified: Persons who have cancer lose weight. Therefore, all persons who lose weight have cancer.

An example of a false assumption is illustrated by the draft of a doctoral dissertation on the breeding of sheep to develop fineness of wool. Unfortunately, the candidate assumed that nothing had been published on this subject in any foreign language. When his dissertation was presented, the Dean of the Graduate College discovered that the subject had already been covered in a German publication. Many months had been wasted in a fruitless duplication of research.

Unfortunately many examples of unwarranted assumptions and illogical reasoning which can be found in library literature have affected seriously the administration of our libraries and their services to scientists. Some case studies illustrate this statement. All of these examples occurred but fortunately not all in one library.

Professor X informed a librarian that his classes had no further use for a certain periodical. The subscription was cancelled and the unbound numbers discarded. Within a few

[3]*Webster's New International Dictionary*, Second Edition (Cleveland and New York, 1950).

weeks Professor Y complained that his students needed this publication for assigned reading. The issues thrown away were out of print and could not be replaced.

A study was made many years ago on the assumption that one could ascertain the type of qualifications needed by reference librarians by listing the questions asked them.[4] The author of this study, a liberal scientist, although he did not claim the title, admitted later that his assumption ignored the fact that many questions which would naturally be asked of a reference librarian are not asked because the patrons know that she would be unable to answer such questions. False conclusions are liable to be drawn as the result of the methods used in questionnaires and interviews, so popular in educational and library circles.

An article some years ago by H. H. Fussler[5] pointed out the fact that the early volumes of scientific periodicals in physics and chemistry were cited to a less extent than recent volumes and that volumes in the English language were cited much more than volumes in foreign languages.

The findings of Fussler were sound but from his study some librarians have without justification drawn the conclusion that the earlier volumes of scientific serials could be safely discarded by large university libraries. This policy might be applied to college libraries[6] and, in some certain fields, to university libraries, but the adoption of this practice by all university libraries would be disastrous to scientific research. Even now the limited holdings of complete sets of some scientific serials have resulted in almost unreasonable demands upon some research libraries for the loan of volumes. An entomologist pointed out that the conclusions drawn by some librarians from Fussler's paper were an excellent example of illogical generalization. Fussler showed that the

[4] W. W. Charters, "College Preparation for Reference Work," *School and Society*, XXVII, 150-152 (1928).
[5] Herman H. Fussler, "Characteristics of the Research Literature Used by Chemists and Physicists in the United States, "*Library Quarterly*, XIX, 19-35, 119-143 (1949).
[6] Andrew A. Shercckman, "A Chemistry Library," *Library Journal*, LXXVII, 1957-1959 (1952).

recent volumes of chemical and physical serials were cited more than the earlier volumes. Therefore, it was argued by some librarians that the recent volumes of all scientific serials were used more than the earlier volumes. The entomologist stated that, in his opinion, entomologists use the earlier volumes of serials more than the recent ones. Librarians should not use Fussler's conclusions to justify widespread discarding of early volumes of scientific periodicals nor should they expect that his study of physical and chemical serials would necessarily hold for all fields of science.

Another conclusion which has been drawn from Fussler's study is that complete sets of scientific serials are not necessary. Many loan librarians have reported that the missing volumes in a set frequently seem to be the ones most called for. Often missing volumes in scientific sets in libraries are for obvious reasons the most valuable and those most needed. That may be the reason why they are lacking.

If a librarian in a large research library believes that Fussler's study should be interpreted as implying that early files of serials and publications in foreign languages are not needed in any research library, then he shows the inability to reach a sound conclusion from sound data.

Another form of error is found frequently in the use of statistics. The number of volumes circulated is considered as a measure of library use. Librarians do not agree on the definition of the terms "volume" and "volumes lent." Is a volume one bound book or a bibliographical entity? Do the words "volumes lent" include only books lent for home use or also books used in the building? And how about the great use of books on open shelves for which no count can be made? Furthermore, does the use of 10 novels equal in value the use of the same number of scientific books which may result in basic scientific discoveries?

Not infrequently a scientist may quote in his own publications, in periodicals or over the radio, information obtained from the use of one book. He may reach thousands of readers but in library statistics this use is counted only as one.

A similar error is found in figuring the cost of cataloging. The total amount of the salaries paid to members of the cataloging department is divided by the number of books cataloged. However, in many libraries catalogers have duties not connected with cataloging. Time studies are necessary to ascertain the amount of time catalogers spend in actual cataloging. Furthermore, the cost of cataloging a single book in English cannot be compared to the cost of cataloging a Slavic or Oriental serial. Unlike figures cannot be compared.

An example of the violation of one of the basic principles of science is the practice of authoritarianism in the administration of libraries. In many libraries policies are decided by the chief librarian without consultation with the scholars and scientists who use the library or even with the heads of the library departments. In some cases no one but the head librarian, and possibly his chief assistant, knows what budget requests are to be made. Science teaches us that truth can be found through verifiable experimentation and experiences, not by dictum by one in authority at the time. It is needless to add that some libraries are administered in the spirit of democracy and with a sincere desire to ascertain through consultations, and when possible through verifiable experimentation, the principles and policies which should be followed by the library concerned.

Incidentally it should be pointed out that the use of the scientific method is not confined entirely to those who are concerned primarily with the physical and biological sciences. Many scholars in other fields such as history, English, social science, and the applied sciences use scientific principles and are in reality scientists in accordance with the definitions used in this paper. Barbara Wootten[7] of the University of London, has made a strong plea for the application of the scientific method to research in the social sciences.

6.

Possibly the most serious result of the lack of scientific background and knowledge among librarians is the somewhat

[7]Barbara Wootten, *Testament for Social Science* (London, 1950), especially Chapters I and II.

general inability to understand the needs of scientists and the importance of satisfying their needs. The principle that "books are for use" is accepted theoretically by librarians, but application of this principle to specific cases seems to be often ignored. In emergencies exceptions must be made to any rule and many library rules should be amended if libraries are to render the service which scientists have a right to expect. University libraries might well consider, from time to time, revision of their rules since conditions change rather rapidly. One library had as its first rule the statement "that there is no rule in this library which should not at times be broken."

Why have many librarians so steadily opposed the establishment of laboratory libraries? A chemist cannot always stop an experiment to run over to the library to look up some publications which should be available in his laboratory. Why cannot more scientists and librarians discuss together some modifications of the highly centralized or the highly departmentalized system in order to ascertain changes which would enable the library to serve its clientele more efficiently than either of the two extremes?

Why do many librarians object to any considerable duplication? Mathematicians who work in different scientific departments often need for almost constant use certain mathematical tables. These tables must be duplicated if the work of the mathematicians is not to be handicapped.

A scientist is engaged with an experiment which is actively underway. He finds he needs a certain book. He is informed by a librarian that "This book is out," "This book is lost," or "This book cannot be found." In so far as requests from research scientists or scholars are concerned, these replies should be outlawed in every research library. If a specialist needs a book immediately for his research, vigorous attempts should be made to supply it. If a book is charged to another reader, he would almost invariably be willing to return the book for emergency use if informed of the need. If a book is lost it is possible that an immediate search would locate it or that another copy could quickly be obtained by purchase or interlibrary loan through the use of the telephone, teletype or telegram. A research worker is not interested in a statement that a book which he must have immediately for completion of an experiment is not available.

If librarians understood why certain publications were needed and the importance of the work being done, their attitude might be different. A knowledge of the bibliographical needs of research scientists might result in changes in buildings, in qualifications required of reference librarians, in the location of books in a library system including the central library, and indeed in some changes affecting the location of buildings on a campus. Too often the location of books, even in a central library, seems to be determined more by library rules and requirements rather than by the bibliographic needs of the scientists.

Another result of the lack of scientific background among librarians is the fact that too few library assistants know the nomenclature used by the scientists and often look entirely blank when information on a scientific subject is needed or when certain publications are requested. One chemist complained that a professional librarian looked in the author catalog in response to his request for a certain volume of "Berichte." She thought the word "Berichte" was an author's name. Another professional assistant asked if "Beilstein" meant bilestone. The head of a large university library asked what was meant by a reference to "Berichte" and "Beilstein." These two publications, Beilstein's *Handbuch der organischen Chemie* and *Chemische Berichte,* formerly *Berichte der deutschen chemischen Gesellschaft,* are possibly the two most used reference publications in the field of organic chemistry. Experience will remedy such elementary errors but in the meantime the lack of knowledge of scientific terms by librarians recently graduated from library schools does not add to the respect for librarians nor, far more important, to the services a library should render to its scientists.

Reference librarians in colleges and universities too often have no reading knowledge of foreign languages. Much scientific research is largely dependent upon German publications. On account of the increase in the use of Russian scientific publications some member of a university library staff should have a reading knowledge of that language.

Unfortunately many scientists have the impression that they can obtain no help from reference librarians. An eminent bacteriologist was complaining of his difficulty in locating certain citations. When asked why he did not consult the reference librarian he replied, "What help could she give me? She hasn't the faintest knowledge of bacteriology and she cannot read German." At a library meeting some years ago a reference librarian stated that reference librarians of a large university could not give assistance to graduate students and faculty members in their major subjects if those subjects were unfamiliar to the reference librarian.

Some librarians state that scientists know their own bibliographies and need no help from librarians. This is another instance of illogical reasoning caused by insufficient contact with scientists. Chemists usually know the bibliographies in their own fields but they do not always know the bibliographies in the allied fields, especially in the biological disciplines which possess extensive and numerous bibliographies. Even a chemist at times may need aid in searching the literature in almost every other branch of science.

It would not be difficult for librarians and scientists working together to make case studies of the difficulties which scientists find in using large research collections. If a sufficient number of such studies were made the results would give valuable data which should result in a marked improvement in the services to scientists.

These comments emphasize the need for a greater proportion of library school students who have both a scientific background and a reading knowledge of some foreign languages.

7.

During recent years the number of library school students with a background in the sciences has been slowly increasing. It is true that the financial returns for scientists are greater in industry than in educational institutions. However, employment in colleges and universities has some advantages, such as permanent tenure, possibly more pleasant surroundings, more opportunities for educational growth through the election of courses in science and languages and through contacts with specialists in many fields of science. In addition, salaries paid librarians with a scientific background have increased rapidly the last few years as the result of the demands of industry.

There is a remedy for the lack of scientific background among those who have already obtained their degrees in the humanities if they are willing to make the effort. Some enterprising librarians, who lacked sufficient scientific background for the positions they were expected to fill, qualified themselves by study and reading. Case studies of some who have made excellent records in scientific libraries can be cited. One assistant who majored in German has qualified herself in the field of medicine by studying at home and taking graduate courses in biology. She is now head of one of the major medical libraries in the country. Another, employed by a large corporation, remedied her lack of scientific background by taking courses in chemistry in the evenings and during vacations and by extensive readings. She has become an outstanding librarian in the field of chemical engineering. Some familiarity with present day science and scientific terms can be obtained by reading the various histories of the sciences, the fascinating books for the laymen which have appeared the last few years, and the Guide Books to the various sciences.

Professors also in the sciences could assist in increasing the number of librarians with scientific background by recommending to some of their students that they consider librarianship as a profession. Some graduate students find it impossible to continue their work for their doctorates. Librarianship offers attractive opportunities for such persons.

Industry usually prefers men for research positions. Library positions, however, offer women with a scientific background and library training excellent opportunities for a fairly satisfactory financial return and, in addition, the possibility of a continuation of their graduate studies if they so desire. More and more women with scientific training have qualified themselves as special librarians in the field of the sciences. Unfortunately, some with scientific training are not used in our larger libraries to the best advantage.

One solution to the problem of providing satisfactory bibliographical services, not only to scientists, but also to scholars in other fields, would be to break down the barriers at present existing between departments in large libraries. A biologist, who is head of a biology library, could serve as a classifier of books in that field, as a specialist in the selection of biological publications, and as an authority on all bibliographical questions in the field of the biological sciences. He could give courses on the bibliography of biology to graduate students majoring in the biological fields. He could also give a course on the history of biology and a first year course on the use of biological literature.

Under this system a library of a university would include on its staff specialists in the various disciplines included in the program of the graduate college.[8] The cost would be considerable but would seem to be justified by the improved service to scientific specialists. Scientific research is expensive. Any reasonable steps to save the time of those engaged in research and to avoid delay in bibliographical investigations would seem to be justified.

As has been pointed out, library schools during the past sixty years have given little attention to science, in spite of its growing importance. Some library schools—unfortunately not all—have started courses in the bibliography and literature of the sciences. Such courses, however, are not yet available at many library schools. Many difficulties, especially in reference work, could be remedied by elementary courses on the literature and bibliography of science, provided students were encouraged to elect such courses. Library school graduates know the most used reference books in the humanities

[8]Herman H. Fussler, "Bibliographer Working in a Broad Area of Knowledge," *College and Research Libraries*, X, 199-202 (1949).

but they do not always know many of the most important reference books in the sciences. Faculties of many library schools do not include any one who has majored in the sciences or who has any considerable knowledge of the bibliography or methodology of science. However, present demand for library school graduates with a greater familiarity with the sciences should in the course of time further affect the organization and programs of the library schools.

Some library administrators have discovered that so much assistance can be obtained from scientists that they have employed them in their libraries although they had no library training or experience. It would be, of course preferable if these scientists had library training. But since a sufficient number of library school graduates with scientific background is not available, positions are being filled with scientists with no library background or experience. Some head librarians have said that for certain positions in their libraries they preferred an applicant with a background in science and no library training to a library school graduate with no scientific background. It is easier to obtain knowledge of library methods than a scientific background with breadth and depth.

Science is international. A noted chemist once said, that the first course in chemistry should be a course in German. Many graduate students in the sciences have been greatly embarrased in the presentation of their theses because of their lack of knowledge of foreign languages. Unfortunately, some library schools have waived the language requirements, and this situation seems to be becoming worse rather than better. In any bibliographic service to research scientists a knowledge of German is essential. One library has urged all recently appointed library assistants with no knowledge of German to elect language courses, and has allowed time for such courses. Every large university library, which is attempting to serve scientists, needs librarians on its staff in sufficient number to make possible the easy translation of publications in every European language, including the Slavic. In the larger university libraries an assistant with a knowledge of the Oriental languages should be available.

8.

Many or most of the scientific departments of a university have their own independent departmental libraries. This situation hinders the scientist in the use of literature in other departmental libraries. It prevents easy communication between scientists and the members of the staff of the central library.

There can be no question that books are needed for ready reference in the various scientific departments of a university. Departmental or laboratory libraries are essential but such collections need not be extensive.

In spite of the increasing interrelationships of the sciences and the dependence of one branch of science on other branches, the present system of departmental libraries tends to isolate the book collections of the library and even the scientists themselves. It cannot be said that only members of a chemistry department can use chemical publications, although some departmental libraries attempt to restrict the use of their collections to members of their own department. Every branch of science has some use for publications in other branches, yet walls are built up among the departmental libraries and also between the university library and the departments of science. The solution is in the hands of the scientists themselves.

One remedy has been proposed by the president of a rapidly growing Southern university, who suggested the establishment of "laboratory libraries" which would make quickly available to the specialist the publications most used by him. These collections need not be large; possibly 4000-5000 volumes would serve the needs of the most exacting department. The larger number of volumes not used frequently should be shelved in the university library together with the duplicates of the books in the laboratory libraries. Such an organization under the administration of the central library in cooperation with the heads of the scientific departments should remedy many of the difficulties found in our present system. Scientists need many books which normally are shelved in several departmental libraries, separated by considerable distances and often on the top floor of buildings.

Under the proposed organization they would find in their own laboratory libraries the ready reference books and periodicals most used in their fields. For other publications they would have only one place—the central library—to visit. Books in the central library urgently needed for temporary use in a laboratory library could be transferred for the time being. Under the present system of departmentalization a bacteriologist, for example, in addition to his use of the publications in the bacteriological department library, would at times need to visit the chemistry, the dairy, the soils, the medical, and the physics departmental libraries, unless there was an enormous amount of duplication.

An alternate organization is now being developed in some universities. On account of the growing relationships between the various branches of the sciences some university libraries have brought together the collections of several closely related scientific departments into one interdepartment library. For example, some biological libraries including both botany and zoology have been organized; other libraries have been combined for the physical sciences. There seems to be a tendency in this direction. The physical and engineering libraries have been combined by at least one university. This arrangement, however, does not provide for the location of a limited number of books for quick reference in the laboratories of the various departments. However, either one of the two systems mentioned above would seem to be far preferable to the customary organization of a number of large departmental libraries.

Since the concept of the scientific method, as used in the physical and biological sciences, is not emphasized or even mentioned in many library schools and less exacting methods of research have been proclaimed in certain branches of the humanities, it cannot be expected that many who have received their training in the humanities will appreciate the need of application of the scientific method to problems of administration. As has been shown, the scientific method has not always been used in published articles and reports in the field of librarianship. If the library schools would emphasize the scientific method—what it is and how it can be applied to librarianship—then the students would obtain a better knowledge of the needs of scientists and the importance of satisfying such needs. Courses in library schools on "Research Methods" should not ignore entirely, as many of them do, the scientific method and its applications.[9] An excellent problem for advanced library school students would be to select masters' essays or even doctoral dissertations in the field of librarianship, professional articles, and other publications on librarianship and point out the false assumptions, fallacies and illogical conclusions.

There are many questions in regard to the use of scientific publications which would justify exploration and the collection of verifiable data by library school students. As would be expected from the lack of emphasis on science in library schools, very few theses are presented by library school students which could be classified as dealing with the physical and biological sciences. Almost all of them are based on the humanities, sociology or education. Out of 81 theses listed in *College and Research Libraries*,[10] as of interest to college librarians, only 6 dealt with questions relating to the physical and biological sciences and the use of publications in these fields. Out of 47 studies listed as under way in this compilation, only three related to the physical and biological sciences. When more students who have majored in science enter the library schools, when more scientists are available to serve as members of library school faculties and in administrative positions in the library world, then the remedy for failures to apply the scientific method will have been found.

9.

Scientists have learned that all scientific concepts are subject to change and redefinition. Librarians are often slow in accepting new concepts, in realizing the importance of

[9] Two recent publications are of special value to library schools interested in the scientific method: Edgar Bright Wilson, *Introduction to Scientific Research* (New York, 1952), and John Oulton Wisdom, *Foundations of Inference in Natural Science* (New York, 1952).
[10] *College and Research Libraries*, XIII, 359-361 (1952).

changes caused by scientific developments, and in adapting library services to these developments. Science was not an important field of activity of universities 100 years ago. In spite of its great development in the last 50 years it is to many librarians still a subject which does not deserve their major consideration in the administration of their libraries and in financial support both for acquisition of scientific publications and for the employment of competent personnel. The new concept of the importance of modern science in our universities is still unknown to too many librarians.

One important fact which librarians can learn from the scientists is the importance of being able to adapt old concepts to altered conditions. To what extent are librarians retaining concepts to altered conditions which should be redefined or abandoned? To what extent are they giving lip service to newer concepts but failing to observe them in the administration of their libraries? A few hundred years ago the first duty of librarians was the conservation of knowledge and the preservation of the records of the past. More recently we have proclaimed that "books are for use" but we have not fully implemented this concept in the administration of our libraries.[11] Several years ago at a meeting of the Association of Research Libraries, during a heated discussion on the restrictions on the use of theses and manuscripts, a noted Japanese visitor whispered to me "I thought that American librarians believed that books were to be used."

May I venture to state that closer relations between scientists and librarians might also aid the scientists. The graduate students in the sciences may not be as inaccurate in their bibliographic citations as are those in many other disciplines but there is still room for improvement.

Far more important, however, is the tendency of the scientist to narrow his field of vision to a point where he is not concerned with related studies. A graduate student once told the instructor in a course on the bibliography of science that he was solely interested in the physiology of one sub-

[11] S. R. Ranganathan, *The Five Laws of Library Science* (London, 1931).

species of the genus Aphis. He did not care about readings in entomology, zoology, or science in general. He could find everything he needed in the *Zoological Record.* After his attention was directed to *Review of Applied Entomology, Biological Abstracts,* and the extensive bibliographies published by the United States Department of Agriculture he realized the extensive relationships of the detailed study he was making.

Librarians who are trying to assist graduate students are too often troubled by the statement: "I can find everything I need in *Biological Abstracts* or *Chemical Abstracts.*" Even experienced scientific bibliographers have difficulty at times in locating articles which are not listed in the commonly used bibliographies. A study now underway at Florida State University[12] indicates that 40% of the citations in certain subdivisions of physiology which are listed in *Physiological Abstracts* (A III of *British Abstracts*), do not appear in *Biological Abstracts.* Many cases could be cited which would indicate that not one of the scientific abstracting journals, valuable as it may be, is complete.

Scientists can also assist on the functioning of libraries by explaining to administrative librarians their needs, and by keeping them informed of their research projects under way. Often more progress can be made by patient conversations than by concise business letters, although the latter method may at times be necessary.

Scientists must concentrate on restricted fields of research but they can also, and many of them do, consider the connotations of their researches. J. B. Conant is an excellent example of an outstanding scientist who has been able to understand and explain the wide ramifications of science. An address by Charles F. Kettering, entitled *The Contribution of Scientific Research to our Society* (not yet published), is another excellent illustration of the contribution scientists can make in the education of laymen.

[12]Mary Nunez Ten Eick, *A Bibliographical Comparison of Twelve Selected Physiological Areas of Biological Abstracts and British Master Paper Physiological Abstracts,* Florida State University (Tallahassee, 1953).

In many universities, scientists and scientific departments should be more active in the consideration of library policies and practices. What proportion of library budget for books, periodicals and binding is allotted to the purchase of publications in the pure and applied sciences and what proportion to the humanities and education? How many departments in the pure and applied sciences are represented on the library committee, as compared with the departments in the humanities? Do all scientific departments have library committees and are they active, not only in their recommendations for publications to be purchased but also in their suggestions for improvements in services to their departments? Are scientists present at meetings of administrative librarians when policies affecting the use of books by scientists are being discussed?

10.

The various assumptions mentioned or implied in this paper should be tested by experimentation. Case studies are needed on the various difficulties which scientists encounter in their use of libraries.

To supply the reference service needed by research scientists in our universities the following desiderata are necessary:

1. Administrative librarians in general should be thoroughly familiar with the scientific method as defined in this paper, its uses by scientists, and its application to librarianship. They should lose no opportunity to inform themselves of the special bibliographic services needed by scientists and should endeavor to make available such services.

2. As an educator every librarian should have a general knowledge of scientific developments during the last 50 years and their effects on our daily lives.

3. University library staffs should include librarians who have acquired through education or experience a general background in the sciences and detailed knowledge in at least one scientific discipline.

4. Members of the staff who have a reading knowledge of foreign languages, including German and in some cases the Oriental languages, should be available to assist scientists.

5. Library schools should give greater emphasis on courses covering the literature of science for all students and the bibliography of science for students who expect to work in college, university or special libraries.

6. A different type of library building and a different arrangement of books within the building are necessary. All publications in a given discipline should be brought together in a special room or section of the Science Room with stacks adjoining for the less used publications in that discipline.

7. A modification of the highly decentralized system of the large departmentalized libraries will be necessary. In view of the increasing number of scientific publications issued each year, this system will fail as the result of the unwieldy size of the collections. Departmental libraries should remain small enough to make their use quick and easy.

Definite progress toward the attainment of these ideals has been made in recent years. More librarians with a background in science are becoming available; library buildings are now being erected with rooms arranged according to readers' interests, as for example, the Science Room, the Humanities Room, etc. This is a step in the right direction but only a step.

The first reaction of librarians to a system such as proposed in this paper, is that it is too expensive—another example of faulty logic. Medical education is very expensive; therefore we should have no medical schools? President Truman's budget for fiscal 1953 included certain items listed as military research adding up to $3,379 million. If to this amount are added the sums spent for research in the United States each year, including the amounts spent by the States, by private universities and by foundations, it will be clear that whatever additional library cost is required to serve science will be proportional.

Before detailed work is started on any scientific project, a search of the literature should be made. Only by such searching can duplication be avoided. Many large corporations realize this fact and have established bibliographic services, which most university libraries do not attempt to supply at present. The lack of such services is a serious hindrance to research in universities. Cost must be considered in relation to the results obtained. It is believed that the services proposed in this paper would be in the end far less expensive than those supplied under our present library organization. In view of the great development of science and the growing importance of scientific research, greatly increased library appropriations will be necessary, if libraries are to furnish adequate bibliographic services to scientists. If larger funds are not obtained, the labors of our scientists will be of limited value and many of the billions of dollars spent in the United States each year will be wasted.

11.

(EPILOGUE)

A somewhat different concept of a library is needed by librarians, as well as by those who use or should use libraries. A library is not simply a building nor is it a collection of books. It is not a group of employees. You cannot define the library in materialistic terms. It is rather a concept—an idea—difficult to express in words. It is a living embodiment of the importance of Truth. It is partly of the intellect and partly of the spirit. It is a powerful stimulus to the discovery of new truths to be added to the store of knowledge it already possesses. It is a positive encouragement to the idea that intellectual development and spiritual growth are possible for anyone who has a desire to keep himself alive both spiritually and mentally. This basic conception of a library which is dedicated to the discovery of Truth and dissemination of knowledge is illustrated by the fact that totalitarians have destroyed many books in libraries and have restricted the use of others. Both scientists and librarians agree on the basic principles of the freedom of the individual, the freedom of research in opposition to authoritarianism and totalitarianism which have no place in science, in librarianship nor, I hope, in America. "Ye shall know the Truth and the Truth shall make you free."

THE CHALLENGE OF AUDIO-VISUAL MEDIA*

Edgar Dale

Research Associate and Professor of Education
Ohio State University

1.

Robert Hutchins once said that the professors of anatomy at the University of Chicago were so specialized that they could not speak intelligently to each other unless they were working on the same parts of the body. The modern library has to face this problem of increased specialized material and it is a difficult one.

There is a sharp increase in numbers of pupils in our schools and students in our colleges. I am not sure that I should call them students. Someone recently asked how many students there were at the Ohio State University. The answer seems to be ten per cent. Nature and wise social philosophy are combining to increase the number of persons attending school and college. About fifty per cent of our young people now graduate from high school. This number will keep increasing as well as the number graduating from college.

The need for international understanding has been thrust upon us through the struggle against world-wide communism. All of us are forced to theorize about communism, its basic dynamism or lack of it, how it can be combatted abroad, how the United States can present to the rest of the world a recognizable and honest image of what we are with all our strength and weakness. How can we combat the caricatured image in which we are shown abroad? This is a problem we also face at home—realistic communication of accurate ideas. Nearly all of us who are a little older are thinking with stereotypes at least twenty years old. The pictures in our heads are of the depression, of capitalism as represented by Sewell Avery.

* A public lecture given at Florida State University, Tallahassee, March 26, 1953.

The truth is hard to come by. It doesn't die but sometimes it lives a wretched life. Reality is often seen through the distorted eyes of envy, the desire to be neutral, to avoid conflict, to refuse to see one's self in a bad light.

A fourth problem which has both bad and good aspects is the abrupt and revolutionary changes that have occurred in mass communication in the last fifty years generally and more specifically in the last ten or fifteen years. The mass newspaper after 1900—mass radio after 1920—mass pictorial journalism after 1935—mass television after 1950.

It is easy to lament the fact that these four problems face us all at once, but this is to be expected. They are part and parcel of the same process. We can sympathize with the old lady who lamented that it was certainly too bad that the depression and all of this unemployment had to come at the same time, but we are stuck with it.

Let us look a little more closely at our first problem. True, there is a Niagara of new information. Yet when we examine it closely we see that it is often technical and scientific information. Indeed, if we examine the expenditures on research at your institution *probably* and at mine *certainly* we see that the studies in human relations are neglected and that we have distorted our research output by putting most of our eggs into the science and technology basket. And more critical still, the research is usually of the kind where you figure out how to pick the fruit more successfully from the tree and not how to plant more and better trees. It is research in better application but not in giving more attention to developing theoretical formulations.

We are, however, not being overwhelmed by either research data or sophisticated observation about how to improve our human relations. How much money are you spending on finding out how children develop, how your students at this university really learn, what their needs are? How much money are you spending trying to discover some new ideas in the science and art of communication?

I do not suggest that science has moved ahead too fast.

Rather our spiritual leg has not kept up with our technological one. We need to speed up the one rather than slow down the other. I like Charles Kettering's story on this point. It seems that a man was planning to catch a train for an important business appointment. The train was due at 9:00 A.M. It came in at 8:45 A.M. He sued the railroad to compensate for the financial loss he had incurred as a result. He lost the suit because the railroad was able to prove that the train was not one half-hour ahead of time but that it was 23½ hours late!

How have we been affected by the sharp influx of students at all age and grade levels? First, it has put a heavy financial drain on communities whose tax structures and methods of collecting taxes were antiquated and unable to meet the problem faced. In the South it has meant a much heavier proportion of the total income has been spent on education than in the North. But it has also brought pupils into the upper grades who ordinarily dropped out. I graduated from high school in 1915 in a class of 17 persons in a high school which had 60 students. Today that high school has over 200 enrolled and the population of the county is no bigger and probably less than it was 37 years ago.

A fairly high proportion of these 17 persons went on to college. Nearly all could have done college grade work. The proportion of the present graduates of that high school who could do acceptable college work is much less. In 1912 parents typically wondered whether their children should go on to high school. Today the problem has been changed and they wonder if they should go on to college. May I point out that in a recent study it was discovered that 42 per cent of the upper fourth of our high school graduates do not go on to college. The problem in a nutshell is that the teacher or instructor today finds youngsters in his classes who 25 years ago would not have gone on. Thus, the upper grades, the high school and the college have at each class level a wider range of abilities represented than has been true before.

2.

I have outlined in greater or less detail some four major

problems with which we must deal—the outpouring of new ideas, new research, increase in numbers in our schools, the need for international understanding, and the problem of mass media of communication. I shall discuss some of these problems in greater detail.

As we look at them we see that they are all related to our modern industrial technology. Without industrialization these problems would never have reached their present proportion. It becomes obvious that we must master the machine before it masters us. We must get ahead of this problem instead of always being behind it. How can we do this intelligently?

I think there is only one answer—to understand and use modern methods of communication—to understand what communication really is. In the Epistle to the Hebrews there is a statement "To do good and to communicate." The new version changes this 17th century meaning of communicate and shifts this line to: "To do good and to share what you have."

If we are to share meanings with each other—and this is our problem—we must have common experiences. The purpose of the common life is to have common meanings. The purpose of the common school is to have common, that is, communicable experiences. Many think that in our colleges we are having specialized experiences before we have had enough general, that is, common experiences. General education is the common education for a common objective, the good citizen.

The grounding for all communication is first-hand, purposeful, concrete, direct experience. It is hard to disagree with what seems a truism yet the history of all education is the breaking out of formalistic meaningless molds, a reaction against dried-up meaningless experience. This is the basic message of most educational reformers—Comenius, Rousseau, Pestalozzi, Dewey, or Kilpatrick. The Great Teacher taught concretely with parables which exposed the formal, ritualistic, meaningless religious rites of the day. There is nothing unclear about what He thought about using your talents, about being a good neighbor, about little children, about forgiveness.

One of the dangers in our common experiences today is

that they relate so closely to machines. To those of us with a rural background such terms as seed, planting, plowing, soil, weeds, winnowing, chaff, straw, crop have rich meaning. A few years ago my son asked me: What is a livery stable?

Today instead of the metaphors of soil and crops we have machine metaphors: dynamics, gears, speed up, momentum, friction, generate, level, etc. Yet machine metaphors have dangers. Man is no machine, let us never forget that. It takes time to grow a man but machines can be quickly manufactured. If a machine goes wrong, you redesign it. If a man goes wrong you start studying what happened 100, 50, 20, 10 years ago. It is difficult to redesign a person as teachers, penologists, and psychiatrists know.

But if fulfillment and growth are the great aims in all education, how can we set up a society where such growth best occurs. I recently read a paper-back book which told the story of three Ann Arbor boys who murdered a nurse. The best word I can use to describe them is to say they were rootless.

The basic structure in a "rooted" society is the family. All of us, as persons and as citizens, must work to see that the family gets a break. As parents we need the wise insights that can come from books, from films, from recordings, from discussions dealing with family life.

Perhaps as librarians you could help families see the importance of tradition, to accept and admire what and where they came from instead of rejecting it, to build pride in the family vacation (planned with materials from your library), aid them in building family hobbies, help them choose recordings, film, and other recreations with more skill.

City children need the same kinds of experience that farm youngsters get through the Four H Clubs. They need summer and week-end camps, to grow gardens, to work on farms. Certainly we can provide opportunities in voluntary agencies for high school students to help out in civic enterprises. Community Chests and Councils have developed such a plan, which is printed in a report of their activities.

But concrete experience isn't enough. We must be sensitive to the ways in which these concrete experiences can be crystallized into workable concepts, generalizations, functional ideas. It is at this point that librarians, supervisors, and teachers need to think more clearly about audio-visual materials and methods. You must think more clearly, for example, than Joseph Wood Krutch who from time to time attacks audio-visual methods of teaching. His attacks are never documented or made specific—a habit unworthy of a scholarly reader which he presumes to be. Thus in the *Nation* for February 26, 1949, he points out to the publishing business that one of the forces they will have to fight will be the "educator and the psychologist, both of whom are increasingly opposed to the printed word." He speaks again of "the educators already strongly prejudiced against books. They are nowadays all committed to audio-visual aids." This, of course is false.

He then goes on to point out what is surely true and what has surely been said by any specialist in audio-visual education who is worth his intellectual salt: ". . . the printed word is still the most generally efficient and effective method of conveying thought or information ever invented by man, and that over the largest of all fields a hundred words is often worth a thousand pictures."

A few weeks ago I wrote an editorial criticizing another article by Krutch. A couple of librarians wrote and said that I had erected a straw man. Let us see if there is a real difference of opinion or whether we are looking at the different sides of the same coin.

Those of us in the audio-visual field (a term that misnames as does the word, librarian) have been concerned about meaningless language, empty abstractions. Our substitute for such language is not a picture but rather rich experiences which are obviously named and discussed. Actually there are few wholly visual experiences in the educational field which we are talking about. There are verbal-visual experiences. The film has a spoken commentary. The film strip has titles, an accompanying manual for the teachers, sometimes a spoken commentary. Even the photographs in the paper or in *Life* have cut-lines.

Written language has a history. In the genetic development of language we first have speech. We speak before we write. And some of us feel that spoken language has been neglected. We think, and I shall discuss this later, that talking-about must precede and surround reading-about. Certainly the words of a play get rich association when one first sees and hears that play.

Hearing experiences may have a warmth and depth that reading experiences do not. But spoken language provides an inadequate record and memory plays bad tricks upon us. Written language can give us accuracy, opportunity for reference, opportunity to go ahead at our own speed and not the speed of a recording, or a film, or a sound film-strip.

I believe that specialists in the audio-visual field would emphasize the huge gap between rich first-hand experiences and the distilling of these experiences into usable concepts and generalizations. Audio-visual materials ranging greatly in concreteness can help us bridge that gap. Thus you will find us discussing first-hand experiences, contrived experiences such as models, drama, field trips, demonstrations, exhibits and museums, television, motion pictures, photographs and film strips, radio and recordings, visual symbols such as maps and charts.

Persons who are verbally facile, and this includes librarians, are often unable to understand how long it takes to grow a good set of concepts. The concept "5" is harder than many first or second grade teachers realize. The concept of *academic freedom* is not easily grasped even by senators. The concept of *scale* on a map is muffed by some adults. Remember, too, that many concepts have names we all know and also other names which may be very like a foreign language to us—names like jejune, feckless, fey, prorogue, manifest, *deus ex machina,* or combo. So it is one thing to master a concept, it is another to master the different languages or words by which these concepts are described.

3.

I mentioned at the outset but did not describe in detail one of the great problems which affect all citizens but particularly those of us who are in the communication business. I refer to the growth of the mass media. Librarians now accept the printed book as a mass medium, but the Duke of Urbino who lived from 1422 to 1482 did not. Here is what Vespasiano in his *Lives of Illustrious Men of the XVth Century* says about a wealthy Italian of that day, the Duke of Urbino:[1]

> We come now to consider in what high esteem the Duke (Frederigo, Duke of Urbino, 1422-1482) held all Greek and Latin writers, sacred as well as secular. He alone had a mind to do what no one had done for a thousand years or more; that is, to create the finest library since ancient times. He spared neither cost nor labour, and when he knew of a fine book, whether in Italy or not, he would send for it. It is now fourteen or more years ago since he began the library, and he always employed, in Urbino, in Florence and in other places, thirty or forty scribes in his services. . . .
>
> In this library all the books are superlatively good, and written with the pen, and had there been one printed volume it would have been ashamed in such company. They were beautifully illuminated and written on parchment.

Well, before too long there were librarians who were not ashamed to have printed books in their libraries. Yet we must remind ourselves of two facts: first, about half of the adults in this world cannot read or write. And second, the average adult in this country has about nine years of education. The older adult has less. The younger adult has more. About 30 per cent of adults are graduates of high schools. About six or seven per cent are college graduates.

Now let me make a point which I'd like to have you think about. Half of our adults are unable to read at a level higher than eighth or ninth grade. Yet much of the serious material dealing with government, economics, politics, world affairs is written at a level higher than this. Every poll dealing with the information of the average adult on foreign affairs shows that about one-third do not even know that a significant world event is taking place, about one-third know about it but can-

---

[1] *The Vespassiano Memoirs* (Lives of Illustrious Men of the XVth Century), by Vespasiano Da Bisticci, Bookseller, Now first translated into English by William George and Emily Waters—Lincoln Mac Veegh (New York, DG 537.8 AiV5) pp. 102, 104.,

not answer many important questions about the event and one-third or less than this of our adults are informed. If we cannot be both ignorant and free, as Jefferson pointed out, what can we do about it?

Should we suggest that these ignorant people read *Time, Newsweek, Harpers?* About 70 per cent of their subscribers have had some college work. *The Reporter* points out that 79 per cent of its readers are college graduates, and of this 79 per cent about 15 or 20 per cent have Ph.Ds.

The question is sometimes asked: Should we bring readers up to the level of these publications or bring the level of the reading material down to the capabilities of the least competent readers? My answer is "Yes" to the former and something else. That something else is for the librarian to look upon himself not merely as an agent for the custody and distribution of printed materials but also as an agency for the custody and distribution of illuminating ideas no matter whether they appear on tape, wax, film, paper or a television screen.

This idea, of course, is one that is highly congenial to the Florida State University Library School. You are offering eleven different audio-visual courses—certainly an indication that you believe in the distribution of ideas by many different vehicles. I am sure that there are dozens of challenges to librarians in thinking through the selection, cataloging, storing, distribution, use and evaluation of these new media—films, filmstrips, recordings, and the equipment to use them.

Yet over and beyond these problems there is another—the wise correlation of these materials with books, with pamphlets, and with guided discussion. Communication in its root meaning concerns itself with sharing. Can we do a good job of distributing ideas unless we concern ourselves with ways in which the ideas one shares with an author can be shared and evaluated by one's friends? Much of the fun of reading a good book is talking it over with others. How can we do this?

As many of the members of this audience know, the American Library Association has received a grant of funds to use in connection with its American Heritage Project. This project involves the training of discussion leaders, the organization of discussion groups meeting eight to ten times, their reading of materials dealing with the American tradition as well as viewing of films, and the discussion of what has been read or seen.

The project has worked well and is being continued with the support of the Fund for Adult Education. People do enjoy discussing what they have read. They like to come to these groups. But the problem of finding good discussion leaders is a difficult one. Our schools and colleges have so emphasized one-way communication that we have not developed a corps of discussion leaders in every community. Teachers do ping-pong questions and answers with their classes. Lawyers lay down the law, preachers preach, and doctors prescribe. I exaggerate, of course, but many of us have not learned to discuss, to entertain an idea. A debate has been described as two liars hollering at each other at the top of their voices. Discussion, I would say, is the conversation of a democracy.

Perhaps librarians do not know of still other reading, viewing and discussion programs supported by the Fund for Adult Education and developed by Dr. Glenn Burch, formerly director of the Film Council of America. One of these programs, "World Affairs Are Your Affairs," involved the use of ten films, ten essays, and ten meetings for the discussion of the films and the essays.

The essays were written by specialists in foreign affairs. The films and essays dealt with world trade, China, Japan, India, Indonesia, Iran, Yugoslavia, Nigeria, England, and with the role of the citizen in world affairs. We experimented to discover whether untrained discussion leaders could successfully handle these materials and we found that they could.

The experimental groups met under the auspices of libraries, unions, churches, schools, youth groups, Americanization classes, and many others. The participants liked the meetings and they wanted more. Dr. Burch is now preparing a discussion program which will be built around the very successful radio series on Soviet Communism developed by the National Association of Broadcasters.

We have talked, too, of developing a series of discussions making use of film strips, believing that these, too, offer a good jumping off spot for discussion. Thus all of the kinds of audio-visual materials in your libraries have been seen as foci or subject-matter for extended study of important problems of the day.

4.

There is one other agency of mass communication with which librarians must deal. I refer to television. Will it be a real competitor for reading time? If so, what kind of reading time will it displace? Will it displace effortless fiction reading or will it displace the reading of important non-fiction, the reading of serious literature? What part will libraries play in using the educational television stations which will be developed?

First, let's realize that one kind of entertainment is always displacing another kind. However, our concern as teachers and librarians should not be with the time-killers but with the time-fillers. How are people fulfilling their needs to grow intellectually and spiritually, to be moving toward maturity? Reading as an agency of self-fulfillment means that it is helping an individual deal more maturely with his tasks as a member of a family, a neighborhood, a town, a state, a nation, the world.

True, relaxation is the necessary counterpart to work and tension. But the nature and the quality of these agencies of diversion are important. Those citizens who help the library with its discussion programs are certainly getting a kind of refreshment from their daily labors. But entertainment is hardly the word for it. The quality of the residue is vastly different.

The test is always—has this experience helped make the

person more mature? Reading a book may either help mature people or arrest them at an infantile level of development. This is true also of television. The issue is not the instrument but the outcome.

We are working today to try to get what I call "choice television"—television run by community educational agencies so as to provide real choices in television. There are 242 educational channels available. Many states are working hard to set up commissions or similar agencies to help take up these channels. Several such stations will soon be on the air—Houston, Los Angeles, St. Louis. My own University will have such a station and we can only hope that it will make the educational contribution of our radio station WOSU.

Where do the librarians come into this picture? I should like to propose a slogan for libraries that may suggest what they can do: YOUR LIBRARY HAS THE BEST IDEAS IN THE WORLD. Through television you will have an opportunity to show the business man, the technician, the farmer, the member of a union, the housewife, the student, the minister just what your resources are. Show parents the kinds of books, reference materials, encyclopedias they should have in their home. Show provocative family discussions about a book, a trip they are planning which uses guide materials from your library. In short, television gives you a show-case in every television home in your community. You can display your wares in their living room.

Will audiences to educational television stations be minority audiences? Of course they will. And don't forget that there are only minority audiences for all television programs. No commercial program regularly presented reaches 50 per cent of the people. The issue always is: What minority audiences are worth while to reach. But don't forget that some of these minority audiences for your more interesting library programs will have 5, 10, 20, yes 50,000 people seeing them.

I would remember always that since your library has in it the best ideas in the world your job in television is to see that these ideas are presented agreeably sometimes, excitingly often, fruitfully always.

5.

The library is in a transitional phase. It is shifting from being a repository of ideas in print to a repository of ideas on film, on tape. It no longer asks the community always to come to it, it goes to them. It is not easy or simple to make this transition. Dr. William F. Ogburn, professor of sociology at the University of Chicago said in a broadcast on December 24, 1944, "My calculations show that it takes, on the average, about five years for an invention to materialize, and sometimes it takes two or three hundred years or longer. All inventions of the past which I have studied have been resisted. . . . We do not get inventions adopted overnight."

It seems to me that great changes whether in schools, in business, in government or in the library pass through these stages: First, Unconscious Inefficiency. We do a poor job and don't know it. Second, Conscious Inefficiency. We know we should do a better job and are conscious of our weaknesses but have not corrected them. Third, Conscious Efficiency. We are correcting our weaknesses but are like the new driver who is overtly conscious of the rules of the road, says to himself, now I do this, now I do that. Fourth, Unconscious Efficiency. We take the new in its stride. The complicated has become habitual. We see no more problem in cataloging, filing, checking out audio-visual materials than we had with books. Getting discussion leaders for our programs is a simple routine. Our television programs are going great guns. Happy Day.

Shall we be pessimists like Hamlet who said: "The time is out of joint, Oh cursed spite, that I was ever born to set it right." Or like Wordsworth say: "Bliss it was in that dawn to be alive, and to be young was very heaven."

THE CHALLENGE OF SCHOOL LIBRARIANSHIP*

FRANCES HENNE
Graduate Library School
University of Chicago

1.

To all librarians, not just school librarians, belongs the major challenge of school librarianship; for this challenge calls upon us as citizens as well as librarians, and cuts across the segments of specialized professional interests. Good school libraries in every school having two hundred or more pupils—that is our major challenge. No library in a school means depriving children and young people of a wealth of pleasurable and profitable experiences with books and other kinds of communications; it means a textbook dominated kind of teaching that defeats the objectives of a sound school curriculum (nor will classroom collections alone save the situation) ; it means the narrowing of learning (and its corollary, the fostering of ignorance), and a negation of the belief in the values that young people obtain from using books and other materials for a wide variety of purposes not directly connected with school assignments.

Public librarians frequently deplore the small percentage of the adult population that uses the public library, the large number of adults who seem to be non-readers, the preference for trivial and mediocre literature that many patrons of the public library display, and similar discouraging conditions. Yet some of these librarians seem to be unaware of, or at least not perturbed by, the absence of libraries in the elementary schools of their own cities. (Some even retard the establishment of libraries in the schools by furnishing deposits of books for the classrooms, and by maintaining or implying that such classroom collections are sufficient for the library

*A public lecture given at Florida State University, Tallahassee, January 30, 1953, under the joint sponsorship of the Library School and the State Conference of Florida School Librarians. This paper was read by Sarah Srygley, of the Library School, Florida State University.

needs of the schools.) Surely, it is no flight of fantasy to believe that many instances of the reading characteristics of adults which librarians deplore might be traced directly to the lack of libraries and of good school library programs in the elementary schools. By the end of the eighth grade, and some feel much earlier, reading habits and library habits are basically formed for a lifetime. The best opportunities for developing the experiences and the attitudes that make the public library users of the future occur in good elementary school libraries. The children's department, for example, usually reaches a relatively small percentage of the school children and tends to attract the better readers. These statements should not be construed as advocating the removal of the children's department from the public library. Elementary school libraries form a very key part in our total library structure, and all librarians should exert every possible influence upon school boards to assume complete responsibility and administrative authority for providing good libraries in the elementary schools.

College and university librarians bemoan the inability of entering freshmen to use a library, and many have found it necessary to introduce a course, incongruous for a college curriculum, on the use of the library and its resources. The source of this problem is in the elementary and secondary schools, and when corrective measures are applied there, the courses for freshmen should no longer be necessary. Most of the entering freshmen have probably come from elementary schools that had no libraries, and many have come from high schools having library facilities that only barely passed accrediting scrutiny or from schools making little or no provision for teaching students how to use the resources of a library intelligently and effectively. The objectives of good elementary school curricula clearly stipulate that the elementary school child have a wide variety of contacts with the school library that enable him to become familiar with using the library and its resources; these experiences should start in the kindergarten, and by the end of the eighth grade the child should have acquired the basic skills and types of information (including many that are taught in the college courses) that he needs when using a library. The high school program builds onto this basic background; it differs from the elementary school experience in degree rather than in direction.

Librarians, along with a good many other people, lament the way children and young people can't read. Although the picture may not be quite so dark as it is generally painted, the instances of reading inabilities and indifferences remain sufficiently high to be of real concern. The provision of libraries in elementary schools, with an active library program and with easily accessible collections of interesting and entertaining printed materials, would contribute immeasurably toward building the reading interests and abilities of young people. All of us get perturbed when we read the findings of some inquirer who has just asked a group of youngsters or of adults some fairly simple questions about history, or political science, or literature, or current happenings. We are shocked by the abysmal ignorance displayed. Should we not be more shocked by the large number of elementary schools that have no books or other materials on recent events and that have pitifully small collections of imaginative literature and nonfiction?

The provision of libraries in schools having 200 or more pupils, then, forms our biggest challenge, and, in a very real sense, this challenge can be modified so that it applies primarily to elementary schools. The typical elementary school has no library, whereas state and regional accrediting standards have brought about the inclusion of a library in the typical high school. As librarians, we should not consider this challenge of the elementary school library solely in professional terms. Our major interests and concerns are those we hold as citizens and as members of a democratic society. We do not want elementary school libraries just because they develop future users of the public library; we do not want them just because they remove or minimize the responsibility of teaching the use of the library in the upper schools and colleges. Important though these factors may be, other considerations carry far greater force: that a good elementary school program depends upon a good library in the school; that easy accessibility to a library in the school contributes in no small way to the shaping of lifelong reading and library habits; that teaching the use of a library and its resources means something more than helping young people acquire a school skill, in that it provides them with information and experience that can later be used profitably in a world flooded with communications; and that the kinds of ideas, facts, and attitudes that the child or young person carries with him from school may be shaped largely by the kinds of books and other materials in the library collection. Classroom collections are in no sense a satisfactory substitute for a school library; they fail to provide boys and girls with the wide range of materials that they need. Students should have access to a school library and to classroom collections of materials temporarily borrowed from the school library.

The school library field has other challenges, too, but before any discussion of them is undertaken, some general observations seem appropriate. Although some challenges apply generally to all school libraries, many do not have this element of universality. A challenge in some schools, some states, or a region might not necessarily be a challenge in all schools, all states, or all regions. Precise definitions of challenges cannot be made easily. In a certain sense, every aspect of school librarianship might be called challenging, and the school librarian daily finds this to be true in innumerable ways. Translating the philosophy of school librarianship into action forms an unbroken line of challenging experiences, those that arise in connection with helping boys and girls and teachers; these instances occur daily in school libraries, and in large measure school librarians meet these challenges with spirit and success. In all probability most school librarians do not think of these daily incidents as challenges, although helping boys and girls to "reach themselves" and working with teachers to achieve the objectives of the school represent challenges of a very high order. On the other hand, most school librarians probably do think of these daily happenings as challanges in a cumulative sense; then they are thinking of school librarianship, and unimaginative indeed would be the school librarian who did not believe his profession to be one of the most challenging in the world.

For many challenges in school librarianship we have tended to use labels other than the word challenge; we are more apt to call them by other names—trends, or new developments, or problems, or headaches. The term "challenge" has an advantage in that it lacks the negative connotation of "problem," and it does not imply actual achievement on any widespread scale in the way that "development" and "trend" quite frequently and erroneously do. All of the terms, however, are misleading in one significant respect. For example, if we are talking about new developments in school library service, there would be, in all reality, only one new development that we would want to hear about, only one meriting special note. That one new development would be that the new developments we have been talking about for ten or twenty or even more years are at long last developing. In like manner, the really biggest challenge we have is to discover why so many challenges that we have been mentioning for so many years still remain unmet and unanswered!

A time for candid appraisal seems to be upon us. If the challenges selected for discussion in this paper tend to be of the problem variety, the still unmet and unanswered challenges, it is not because the writer elects to carp or to stress the negative rather than the positive. All of us recognize the strides that have been made in school library development since the turn of the century; yet honesty compels us to admit that we cannot feel smug about the distance still remaining between the goals we have set for school libraries and the present status of achievement of those goals. We can no longer, it seems to me, afford to rationalize that school librarianship still remains in a pioneer stage in many respects, or that time lags must inevitably occur between the formulation of objectives and the achievement of objectives. If we rationalize too much in these and similar terms, we may lose valuable time and opportunities; and, even worse, we may misdirect our thinking and our efforts.

2.

For many years our professional writings and our discussions in meetings, workshops, and conferences have described the basic philosophy and the approved procedures for school library service. The literature is not a static literature, and it is remarkably free of the so-called ivory tower theories. To reconcile the lag between our definition of good school library service (as expressed in our written and spoken communications) and the actual practice of school library service in the country as a whole poses a singularly difficult task. It would be foolish to maintain that we have all the answers about school libraries or to believe that we will not develop new ideas and procedures; but it is equally foolish not to admit that before we can develop new ideas and new procedures, we must put many of our present beliefs into operation and thereby test and evaluate them.

When we examine the literature of school library service and when we recall discussions at professional meetings, we note that certain areas or aspects of school library service have repeatedly been emphasized as major developments or key challenges, in school librarianship. Six subjects that have received considerable attention include the following: the provision of libraries in elementary schools, the school library as the materials center in the school, making the school library truly accessible to students in the school, the provision of adequate staff, effective guidance services in the library, and policies and procedures affecting the selection of books and other materials. The challenges associated with the provision of elementary school libraries have already been noted in this paper; those of the remaining five topics will be summarized briefly.

The school library *is* a materials center. Whether we call the library a library or a materials center makes little difference, and only a semantic difference in any event. If our school libraries, however, are not functioning as materials centers, a very serious difference results. The objectives of school libraries clearly state that the library should be the center for all the printed and audio-visual materials in the school, and that the librarian should have the administrative responsibility for acquiring, housing, and distributing all materials. These materials include three main categories:

(1) trade books, magazines, pamphlets, and newspapers (2) audio-visual materials, and (3) textbooks. Although exceptions can be found in many schools, most school libraries do not function as materials centers. Many school librarians have worked vigorously to keep their school libraries from becoming materials centers. If we explore the reasoning of this group of librarians, we usually find the fear (and frequently a very plausible fear) that the assumption of responsibility for audio-visual materials and textbooks will mean extra work of a clerical and technical nature for the librarian, with no additional help provided. The reasons for centering all materials in the library are numerous, valid, and well known to us; it must be stressed, however, that the library cannot operate as a materials center unless sufficient staff (both professional and clerical), sufficient funds, and sufficient space are provided. Statements to the effect that school librarians have missed the boat on the audio-visual program and that it will not be too easy for us to redeem ourselves have much truth in them. Although many leaders in the audio-visual field are articulate and vigorous exponents of the library's being the center for audio-visual materials, an equally large number oppose this theory and remain strongly possessive about their wares. Our challenge consists mainly of influencing three groups by persuasion: to convince many school librarians and many audio-visual materials specialists of the advantages of having the library serve as the materials center in the school, and to persuade many administrators to provide the adequate machinery for administering a real materials center in the school. The advantages to teachers and students, resulting from the location of all materials in one center, merit all our efforts.

Not only should the school library be the center for audio-visual materials to be used throughout the school, but use of audio-visual materials should also be made within the library itself. We theorize, and rightly so since the year is 1953, that on many occasions librarians can best meet the needs of students by recommending a film, or a filmstrip, or a recording. Many school libraries have equipment that enables students to listen individually to a wide variety of audio materials, but school libraries having viewing or projection cubicles for individual use remain relatively rare.

Within the last decade, school librarians have been re-examining the challenge of making the library functionally accessible to students and to teachers within the school. Four developments that have resulted seem particularly noteworthy: the growing practice of having elementary school students come to the library in ways other than the traditional library class periods; the renewed interest in the program of scheduling junior and senior high school students to libraries rather than to study halls; the recommendations that schools having 2,000 and more pupils (1,000 and more if the library serves as a study hall) have two or more libraries (multiple libraries); and the increasing number of schools providing library service during the summer months.

The practice of scheduling elementary school classes for regularly assigned "library hours" has become firmly established in many schools, and the more meaningful, more functional, and more elastic program of having teachers come to the library with their classes when the need to use the library's resources occurs naturally in the course of instruction is not yet found on any widespread scale. The non-scheduled program (rigidly scheduled for the entire semester, that is, since the librarians for obvious reasons must know reasonably well in advance when a class will come to the library) also permits greater use of the library by individual students and by student committees coming from the classroom to obtain library materials for immediate needs. Too, the non-scheduled program provides ample opportunities for individuals and groups to use the library in connection with their non-academic reading. The circumstances under which the non-scheduled program flourishes—a curriculum not dominated by textbook teaching, teachers willing to relinquish that free hour when they turn their students over to the librarian, and a librarian prepared and willing to integrate the library with the school's educational program—do not always exist. The librarian wanting to introduce this type of program may find a real selling job confronting him in his school.

In connection with this subject of making the elementary school library as accessible as possible to students, mention should also be made of the necessity to correct a very common and very unfortunate practice, that of keeping kindergarten, first grade, and second grade pupils out of the school library. That school library experiences should start with the kindergarten (and earlier if the school has nursery or pre-school classes) and should continue thereon seems too obvious a point to belabor.

Mention of the library-study hall for junior and senior high schools brings cries of distress from most school librarians, and in view of the conditions surrounding many existing study-hall library situations, one cannot blame librarians for their fears and suspicions. The study hall, bleak and having few, if any, books, can quite properly be called a relic of an educational program that operated on the theory that textbooks contained all the printed material that students needed for the preparation of their lessons. Today, in view of the nature of approved instructional methods, of the content of the curriculum, and of the varied interests and abilities of students, a study hall no longer makes sense, and we hear school administrators and teachers voicing this opinion with increasing frequency. If, however, all study in junior and senior high schools is to be done by students in a library environment, certain conditions must be met without fail; otherwise the objectives of such an arrangement will not be achieved and the library will become a study-hall rather than a library. Adequate size of library staff, adequate library space, and carefully planned, systematic scheduling of the study hours in the students' programs become imperative.

Although multiple libraries for schools having 2,000 students (1,000 students if the library serves as a study hall) have been specifically recommended since 1945 in *School Libraries for Today and Tomorrow*[1] (generally interpreted as a state-

---

[1] *School Libraries for Today and Tomorrow; Functions and Standards*, Committee on Post-War Planning, American Library Association (Chicago, 1945).

ment of national standards for school libraries), relatively few schools of this size have achieved the status of having two or more libraries. Until these standards are met, the library facilities in the schools affected remain inadequate and functionally inaccessible to students and teachers. The incongruity of the current situation can be readily apprehended when we compare the library facilities of large elementary and secondary schools with the library facilities of colleges of similar size (or, for that matter, with many colleges having far fewer than 2,000 students). This comparison becomes even more significant if we keep in mind that the demands placed upon the school library are more numerous and more varied than those placed upon the college library.

The number of school libraries that are being kept open during summers increases, particularly in elementary schools. Local circumstances usually determine the feasibility or desirability of this practice. In communities having no or inferior public library facilities, keeping the school open during summer provides a much needed service; in schools having summer programs of any kind, the library forms a natural part of that program.

Demonstration and tested practice are sorely needed for many aspects of library accessibility so that we may have sound and workable plans for making school libraries functional and easily accessible. This holds true not only for the four types of library service just described, but also for other developments in school library organization that are related to the general subject of accessibility, such as library facilities and services for twelve grade schools, for consolidated school districts, and for schools having less than 200 students.

3.

A fourth key challenge in school librarianship, obtaining sufficient staff for school libraries, has been of grave concern to us for a very long time. Our national standards represent minimum standards for size of staff, professional and clerical, and yet how far we remain from achieving these minimum standards on any widespread scale. Indeed, many people continue to believe that the standards for size of staff are too visionary; apparently they also believe that there is something fundamentally right about school librarians overworking themselves. (Again, comparing size of staff in school and college libraries proves illuminating.)

In a recent discussion of this problem a school administrator said that adding more student assistants (unpaid student assistants, that is) to the library staff would solve the problem; unfortunately, many others hold this same viewpoint. Historically, the student library assistant program has accounted in large measure for the lack of sufficient professional and clerical staff in school libraries today. The policy of having student library assistants has much merit, but student assistants take extra time and mean extra work for the librarian, if the student assistant program has the educational values that we want it to have for the students. For some kinds of work in the library (dusting, mending, and shelving books, to name a few), students, if they are the ones who do these chores, should receive pay, since these janitorial and clerical activities have no intrinsic educational worth, and cannot be justified on the basis that they constitute school service for which no monetary payment should be made. Small comfort can be derived when the librarian's load is relieved of janitorial and clerical tasks at the cost of student exploitation.

Regional technical processing centers have been recommended as one method for relieving the school librarian of many technical and clerical burdens, which now consume time that should be devoted to working directly with students and teachers. Although technical processing has been centralized in one office or headquarters in some city, county, and unit school systems, many other school systems have not yet achieved this goal. One state provides some centralized processing services for schools in the state. The development of regional processing centers, involving cooperative agreements among several schools in several school districts, remains essentially in the paper stage. Here again we need demonstrations and experiments so that proposed plans for these centers can be tested and improved.

We are speaking now of providing school libraries with sufficient professional and clerical staff so that the school librarians will have time to meet the requests and needs of students and teachers, to participate in curriculum planning, and to do all the many other things that a good school expects from its library program. Until we have sufficient staff and sufficient materials, we cannot fully achieve our stated objectives for school library service. When we have attained ideal working conditions, perhaps then we dare to raise another question (one that applies to all libraries)—can arrangements be made for the librarian (the materials specialist) to have some time during his working week to familiarize himself with the contents of new books and other materials?

In view of the critical shortage of school librarians, it may seem preposterous to stress standards and objectives that recommend increasing the size of library staffs in many if not most schools, on a basis of one trained librarian for every 500 students (a part-time or preferably full-time librarian in schools having 200-500 students) and one clerical worker for every 1,000 students (a full-time clerical worker in schools having 500-1000 students and part-time clerical assistance in schools of 200-500 students). The urgent necessity to recruit school librarians cannot be emphasized too strongly; the insufficient number of available school librarians presents us with a serious challenge that has almost reached the proportions of a crisis. At the same time, we cannot afford to compromise our standards because of these conditions. Not only must we strive to recruit and to train librarians for the positions that are now available, but we must also not relinquish our efforts to increase the number of available positions, whether it be new positions created in schools introducing a library program or new positions created in schools wanting to meet minimum standards for size of library staffs. Parenthetically, it should be noted that the activities and the atmosphere of adequately staffed school libraries might exert considerable influence in attracting young people, teachers, and others to the school library profession.

4.

Limitations in size of staff have worked a particular hardship upon the guidance program in the library. Knowing the content and uses of books and other materials forms the librarian's major responsibility and major contribution. The application of this knowledge, however, involves a variety of guidance services; in addition, the school librarian, being a teacher in the school and being in charge of a part of the school that is unique and distinct in the kinds of experiences that it offers young people, frequently has opportunities and responsibilities for counseling young people in ways that may not be directly related to the use of books and other materials.

These guidance services are stated or implied in the objectives of school library service, and they have been described in some detail in the literature on school librarianship. Aspects of the guidance program that currently seem to be receiving the most attention involve the following activities on the part of the librarian: participating in curriculum planning; helping teachers to become familiar with standard guides in the evaluation and selection of materials; reporting to teachers and guidance counselors characteristics of students observed in the library; providing opportunities, when appropriate and helpful, for maladjusted students to work as student assistants in the library; making full use of the many opportunities which the library presents for helping young people to think and to behave in ways befitting members of a democratic society; implementing a program of teaching the use of the library and its resources that is closely integrated with classroom instruction and that is planned by a committee representing all departments of the school; working closely with teachers in guiding the reading of students having reading difficulties; helping students in the selection and use of books and other materials, and in developing reading interests and tastes; and working intensively with one or two students a year in an effort to help them overcome some common garden variety type of reading problem.

These all-important services of the librarian contribute substantially and positively to the education of youth; they take time, however, and all too often they get brushed aside so that other services and routines of the library may be performed. The challenge facing us here is an important one, and includes not only the problem of library staffing but also the need for a re-evaluation of the goals and the emphases now predominating in many school library programs.

5.

The sixth major challenge in school librarianship selected for mention in this paper pertains to policies and procedures for the selection of books and other materials. Four developments in this broad area will be noted, and these but briefly—censorship, the quality of book selection, materials centers, and expenditures for materials.

We are acutely aware today that some individuals and some groups strongly advocate a rigidly controlled censorship of materials for the schools. Every effort to resist these pressures should be exerted. We should also guard against those influences that in no sense can be called censorship but that may affect the quality of the books and other materials selected for the schools. In some schools high pressure salesmanship may lead principals, teachers, and even librarians into buying books of very poor quality. A keen awareness of the schools as a potentially huge market for books and other materials exists today, and the competition for this market will be brisk to say the least. Influences of another kind that frequently lead to the purchase of mediocre books for school libraries can usually be traced to the zeal of librarians and teachers to get students to read anything. Rewritten classics, most so-called teen age fiction, and many poorly written books on themes or subjects that appeal greatly to young people are cases in point.

Many of these undesirable influences or tendencies can be checked in one or more of several ways: having libraries in schools, delegating responsibility to the librarian for final decisions on the selection of books and other materials, having standards of book selection that recognize the principle that no mediocre book ever served any purpose better than a good book and that good books for children and young people exist in abundance; and the development of materials centers where teachers and librarians may examine books and other materials.

Principals, teachers, and librarians have expressed a very marked interest in these materials centers, and many centers have recently been established. Ideally, no teacher should be more than fifty miles distant from a materials center where he could examine trade books, textbooks, courses of instruction, and other kinds of material, and from this examination decide on the materials to be used in connection with the classes that he teaches. To be functional the centers must be reasonably comprehensive in coverage of materials (and should not be developed on the premise that publishers should send sample copies), and under the direction of a materials specialist. One of the major purposes of the centers is that of keeping teachers and librarians informed about new publications, and of eliminating the numerous risks now encountered in buying books and other materials sight unseen. For over a decade now we have also been talking about other kinds of materials centers—regional centers, and possibly a national center, that would be fairly definitive in coverage and that would offer a wider range of bibliographic services than would the local materials centers. In due time we can expect to see vast improvements in the bibliographic apparatus or machinery dealing with materials for elementary and secondary schools—in the consolidation and improvement of the now widely scattered and frequently incomplete reportings and evaluations of new materials, in the analyses of materials, and in the utilization of the many new devices and techniques that have been developed by the specialists in bibliographical organization.

In the final analysis, appropriations most affect book selection, and our constant concern centers upon the woefully small amount of money that most schools in this country spend for library books. Recent reports from 107 school systems show the following median expenditures per pupil for library books: elementary schools, $0.65; junior high schools, $0.89;

senior high schools, $1.10, and all grades, $.089.[2] Although these figures are disheartening, they seem sizable in comparison with the expenditures for library books in those schools in the sample that fall below the median, and no doubt they would assume relatively colossal proportions if one had the figures for expenditures in all the schools in the country for comparison. The overall challenge of motivating schools to allocate sufficient funds for the purchase of library books belongs not just to school librarians; it belongs to the American people. In these days when schools are being asked to economize and when many administrators are looking at the library budget as a possible place for cutting expenditures, we must take advantage of every possibility to inform and to convince schools and communities of the essentiality of school libraries in the education of youth. A library is a basic and natural part of a school; it is not a frill.

6.

These challenges pose complex problems, but slowly and steadily advances are being made to overcome them. Many of the ways and methods that school librarians are using to resolve these problems constitute in themselves new and important developments in school librarianship. Techniques for evaluating school libraries have been improved, and an increasing number of schools are evaluating library services and facilities in terms of objectives. In some states standards for school libraries are being revised, and state standards for elementary school libraries are also being formulated. The number of states, cities, counties, and consolidated districts having school library supervisors or consultants slowly grows larger. The work of these supervisors and consultants in extending and improving school library service cannot be praised too highly. The news about the professional training of school librarians is encouraging, and the time does not seem far distant when some general agreement will be reached that recognizes the principle that the professional training of

[2]"Per Pupil Expenditures for Instructional Materials and Supplies, 1950-51, in 107 School Systems," *Educational Research Service*, Circular No. 10, 1952, National Education Association, American Association of School Administrators and Research Division (Washington, 1952), p. 2.

school librarians should parallel the professional training of the other teachers in the schools. The efforts to have courses dealing with books and other materials for children and young people incorporated in the professional training of teachers are slowly meeting with success; as are the endeavours to acquaint prospective teachers and administrators with the objectives and functions of school libraries. The inclusion of a basic collection of books and other materials for children and young people in the libraries of teacher training agencies is indispensable in the preparation of teachers; this principle is gradually being recognized and acted upon.

More and more, school librarians are attending state, regional and national professional meetings and conferences of school administrators, curriculum directors, and classroom teachers. In so doing the librarians keep informed about school developments and they also have numerous opportunities to bring library services and materials of instruction to the attention of administrators and teachers. Active participation of librarians in state or regional plans for the improvement of schools, such as those now going on in Illinois, New England, and elsewhere, contribute significantly to the improvemen and development of library programs in the schools.

The school librarians' own professional organizations, both national and state, are growing in size, in stature, and in influence. These groups work continuously for the improvement of school library services and for the extension of school library facilities.

Even though the gains we have made in meeting the challenges of school librarianship bring us no complacency, in view of all that remains to be done, they nevertheless do bring returns rich in reward; for the worth and the significance of the school library in the educational program of the school and in the lives of boys and girls and young people cannot be overstressed, and each inch of progress carries with it untold benefits.

THE CHALLENGE OF LIBRARY LITERATURE TO EDUCATION FOR LIBRARIANSHIP, 1923-1953*

LOUIS R. WILSON
Professor of Library Science
University of North Carolina

1.

In dealing with the challenge of the literature of librarianship to modern librarianship, my major purposes are to show: (1) what the status of library literature was in 1923 (2) how it limited the education for librarianship programs of that day (3) what the nature and extent of its growth in the past three decades have been (4) what its present status is; and (5) how it inevitably affects the preparation of librarians of the future. In considering the subject I shall not undertake to treat it exhaustively, but on the contrary, what I shall say will be in the nature of a commentary on certain of its most significant aspects.

2.

The present day library school student may well take with a grain of salt the statement that his predecessor in 1923 could almost count on the fingers of his two hands the number of titles of important professional library textbooks and journals which he would have to master in order to qualify for a successful career as a professional librarian. His skepticism would be altogether natural. Today with all of his hours crowded with constant reading not only about books in the humanities, the social sciences, and technology and science, but especially in books and journals in the field of librarianship, he certainly has little in his present experience to justify him in giving full credence to such a pronouncement.

The facts, however, are against him, or largely so as far as the date 1923 is concerned. That year definitely marked a

*A public lecture given at Florida State University, Tallahassee, March 19, 1953.

turning point, and since then the amount of time the student has had to spend upon the literature of librarianship has steadily grown until now it is seemingly impossible for him to read everything that has appeared and is appearing in the field.

The American Library Association was well aware of the situation in 1923. Its members had recently studied carefully the Williamson *Report* on the library schools of the day and knew that among the many limitations they were confronted with was that of adequate materials upon which to base a sound educational program. The appointment of a Temporary Library Training Board in 1923 to survey the general field of education for librarianship and of a permanent Board of Education for Librarianship in the year following was aimed at the stimulation of better teaching materials as well as at the establishment of higher standards, the employment of better trained faculty members, the provision of greater financial support for library schools, and the association of library schools with degree-granting universities.

Mudge's *Guide to Reference Books*, the *Dewey Classification*, parts of the *Library of Congress Classification*, the *Library Journal*, *Public Libraries*, the *Wilson Bulletin*, the *A.L.A. Bulletin*, a number of the H. W. Wilson Company indexes and catalogs, *Publishers Weekly*, and *The New York Times Book Review*—these titles, with national bibliographies and the publications of the Library Bureau, the R. R. Bowker Company, and the office of the U. S. Office of Education, constituted the core of professional literature with which the library school student had to deal.

Such a limited literature, devoted almost exclusively to the housekeeping aspects of librarianship, provided a correspondingly limited foundation for a broadly based curriculum. Consequently, when in 1926 the Board of Education for Librarianship requested the Association of American Universities to indicate the type of degree it would recognize as an appropriate credential for the completion of a one-year library curriculum imposed upon a bachelor's degree, the Association replied that a second bachelor's degree was all that it could allow, and that its actual preference was a certificate in library economy. The inadequacy of the degree was thus made to match the inadequacy of the literature of the subject, the poor administrative organization and financial support of the schools, and the limited qualifications of their faculties.

3.

Nineteen twenty-four witnessed a decisive change in library interest and in a corresponding growth in library publications. Three organizations were principally responsible for this. They were the American Library Association, the American Association for Adult Education, which was established in 1924, and the Carnegie Corporation of New York, which in 1925 embarked upon a dynamic program of library stimulation.

The American Library Association, responding in 1925-26 to the stimulation of extensive grants from the Carnegie Corporation for education for librarianship, for library extension, and for adult education, established boards to develop those interests and set them to preparing a series of publications in those fields for its fiftieth anniversary in 1926. For that occasion, it carried out a national survey of all types of libraries, and reported the results in two notable volumes. Its Board of Adult Education projected a series of *Reading with a Purpose* publications and produced a major report entitled *Libraries and Adult Education*. The Board of Library Extension likewise issued a detailed statistical report entitled *Library Extension,* and the Board of Education for Librarianship completed its first comprehensive study of the library schools and published its first codification of *Minimum Standards.* The *A.L.A. Catalog,* revised and enlarged for the occasion, was also published and widely distributed and rounded out an important addition to the professional resources of the day.

The American Library Association, through the Board of Education for Librarianship, also undertook to improve teaching in library schools through the preparation of a series of texts in the fundamental subjects of the curriculum. It placed a specialist in the field of curriculum revision in charge of this undertaking and set a number of experienced librarians to work in the preparation of texts to take the place of the notes which individual teachers had previously been required to prepare for themselves. Texts on circulation work, by Flexner; reference work, by Wayer; book selection and book ordering, by Drury; and cataloging, by Miss Mann were issued in rapid order, each covering a specific field systematically, thereby making it possible for library school instructors to dispense largely with detailed lectures from notes and to emphasize special aspects of subject matter which required special consideration. While some of the texts proved somewhat unsatisfactory and have been superseded in recent years, they appeared at a time when on account of the limited number of students in library schools it was impossible for librarians to produce texts unaided.

The second event which stimulated library interest and brought into being a new series of publications which demanded consideration by librarians was the establishment of the American Association of Adult Education in 1924. This Association inaugurated a vigorous program of publication. It established *The Journal of the American Association of Adult Education,* projected a series of *Studies in Adult Education* featuring the results of research in adult reading, and prepared handbooks for the guidance of adult education workers in thirty or more fields, including libraries. *The Public Library: The People's University,* by Johnson, pointed up the role of the public library in the movement, stimulated the American Library Association to step up the tempo of its *Reading with a Purpose* series, and promoted the provision of readers' advisory services in libraries. The publication by the Association of the results of research in different aspects of reading also threw new light upon the role of print in the continuing education of adults.

Waples and Tyler, in *What People Want to Read About,* devoted their attention to the subjects about which different elements in the population were interested in reading. Through careful research they identified the reading interests of the public library's varied clientele. Gray and Munroe undertook to discover the actual reading ability of the average American and came up in *Reading Interests and Habits of Adults* with the disconcerting fact that reading was a very difficult undertaking for the average citizen because he possessed the reading ability of only a sixth-grader. Then Gray and Leary, in their work *What Makes A Book Readable,* went on to discover what elements in writing make for ease or difficulty in reading, their work leading ultimately through the studies of Lorge and of the Readability Laboratory of Columbia University to the preparation of a series of volumes published in *The People's Library* which librarians hoped would lessen the difficulty of the poor reader in comprehending what he read. Thorndike, of Columbia, was put to work investigating the truth or falsity of the adage that an old dog couldn't be taught new tricks, or, that as an individual became older, his ability to learn decreased almost to the vanishing point. The results of his study, published under the title *Adult Learning,* showed that while the period in which it was easiest for an individual to learn was when he was from 16 to 24 years of age, it was possible for him to continue to learn throughout his entire life though with increasing difficulty.

These publications furnished a sound foundation for work in the field of adult education, thereby contributing to the conviction that the library, whether school, college, university, or public, was an educational agency in its own right altogether capable of contributing to the diffusion of knowledge and therefore fully entitled to public support as a significant educational institution.

The role of the Carnegie Corporation in this development was four-fold. It aided the American Library Association financially in greatly extending its work in adult education, in library extension, in education for librarianship, and in publication. It provided the stimulus and financial support for the establishment of the Graduate Library School of the University of Chicago and for the support of the School of Library Service of Columbia University and other library schools. And in the late 1920's it set up the College Library Advisory Committee for the stimulation of interest in the four-year liberal arts college libraries, thereby initiating work for the next ten years in the improvement of college libraries generally. Its activities in this field resulted in the publication of *College Libraries*, by Randall; *Principles of College Library Administration*, by Randall and Goodrich; *The College Library Building*, by Gerrould; *A List of Books for College Libraries*, by Shaw; *A List of Books for Junior College Libraries*, by Morhardt, and a number of booklets and articles by Bishop and other members or associates of the College Library Advisory Committees on various aspects of college library administration.

4.

While the publications mentioned above covered a wider range of interest than library publications did prior to 1923, they nevertheless dealt primarily with the activities of libraries. Their scope was broader, but they remained library centered and were little concerned with educational and social movements in general. Beginning in 1930, however, publications in other fields began to influence librarianship profoundly. This was strikingly true of publications in the fields of education and the social sciences. In 1933 under the editorship of Ogburn and Odum, the President's Research Committee on Social Trends issued the highly important work *Recent Social Trends in the United States*. This two-volume survey of the social forces at work in the nation and the special monographs on education, on inventions, on government, on population changes, and similar subjects, by which it was accompanied, focused the attention of librarians upon the role of the library as a social institution. Library schools began to list courses in their curricula on the library in the community or the library as a social institution, and the Graduate Library School of the University of Chicago went so far as to offer a course on library trends. The library schools sensed for example, as they had not previously, that the study of such a subject as population had implications for libraries; that the composition of the population in states such as South

Carolina and California, in which the ratio of children of school age to adults varied greatly, might have a direct effect upon library practice. For example, in South Carolina the ratio of children of school age to adults was one to one, whereas in California it was one to two. In the light of such simple ratios, it was clear that when the public librarian in South Carolina selected books for his clientele, he should be an expert on books for children and that a comparatively large number of persons should be trained in that State to administer school libraries. This is because there are as many school children as there are adults. Furthermore, one-third of the children use the public library once a month, whereas only one-tenth of the adults use it that often. In California, on the contrary, books and adult education programs for grown-ups would call for principal consideration since the adult population is twice as large as the school population. From a careful examination of *Recent Social Trends* and other social studies, it became apparent that the multiplication of subjects in the school curriculum, the size of governmental units, the invention of the automobile and radio and other developments of this nature had a direct bearing upon the library, and that if the library attempted to adjust itself properly to the changes effected, it would be compelled to understand clearly what the implications of the situations were.

Three examples of social movements in the early 1930's which greatly stimulated thinking concerning the library in the social order were (1) the depression (2) the setting up of the National Resources Planning Board, and (3) the establishment of schools and departments of public administration in American universities.

The depression, spreading its scourge over the nation in the early 1930's brought the public library into a prominence it had never known before as an educational and recreational agency and as an emergency employer of persons on relief. It sent throngs of the unemployed to library reading rooms everywhere, and it rapidly brought into being a type of library service that in some sections of the country greatly contributed to the subsequent establishment of public libraries and evoked a considerable number of reports and publications on public library development. It emphasized the importance of the equalization of service whether in schools or libraries and led to increased activity in library extension and publication through state aid.

The establishment of the National Resources Planning Board by the Federal Government set off a nation-wide chain-reaction in planning. State planning boards sprang up everywhere and began to study intensively the development of their physical resources and to publish the results of their investigations in numerous reports. Library planning at the national and state levels followed, the American Library Association issuing its *National Plan for Libraries* in 1935, with librarians in 45 states issuing state plans by the end of 1936. Post war planning for all types of libraries followed as a natural step after World War II, bringing into being such notable titles among others as *National Plan for Public Library Service*, by Joeckel and Winslow, and *School Libraries for Today and Tomorrow*, by Douglas.

The general provision in the 1930's of courses in educational administration, public administration, and industrial management in departments or schools of education and public and business administration in the universities of the nation, led to the close scrutiny of theory of administration and its application in those fields. Numerous treatises appeared on the elements and principles of administration in these subjects and were studied in turn by librarians and were applied to all phases of librarianship. Thus the writings of Cubberly and Strayer in educational administration, of Merriam, Gulick, White, and others in the field of public administration, and Keynes and Slichter in industrial administration, were followed by Joeckel and the McDiarmids, by Miles and Martin, by Wilson and Tauber, by Randall and Goodrich, by Lyle, Miss Herbert, Wight, and many other librarians on various phases of library administration. In fact, the subject of library administration profited tremendously from contributors from within and without the profession and can be studied by the prospective librarian with the assurance that it will meet his major needs if it is constantly added to through research and current publications.

5.

Investigation in public, industrial, and educational administration not only influenced publication in library administration but stimulated studies and publications in other aspects of librarianship. The library schools which offered graduate work leading to the M.A. and Ph.D. degrees in librarianship have responded to this challenge and in the past two decades have produced an extensive body of literature in which the results of investigations, surveys, and critical studies have been recorded. This development has, from many points of view, been especially important and salutary, since library situations and practices have been subjected to careful observation and evaluated in accord with approved standards.

Three types of publication may be attributed to this development. Of these, the most obvious and, from the practical standpoint of library administration, the most important, have been the reports of surveys of college, university, and public libraries. The studies of college libraries by Randall and Morhardt; of university libraries by Wilson, Kuhlman, Coney, Tauber, Jesse, Orr, and others associated with them; of public libraries by Joeckel, Carnovsky, Wight, and their associates; of regional libraries in the Pacific Northwest and the Southeast; and of public libraries throughout the nation by Leigh and his collaborators, have dealt with many phases of librarianship and have supplied specific illustrations of how actual practice may be made to conform to approved standards. The reports growing out of these studies have not only acquainted librarians and library school students with actual library practice, but they have also shown how standards can be applied and procedures can be recommended to insure improved administration. These publications have greatly aided university and city administrators in establishing proper administrative financial policies for libraries at a time when such administrators were being confronted with staffs and book collections which had doubled in a relatively short period of time.

The publications growing out of the Public Library Inquiry have had an additional value. They have dealt comprehensively with the whole public library movement in the United States from its inception to the present, and they make clear the nature of the contribution of the public library to American democracy. They show that the public library, while not patronized by a majority of American citizenry, has stood for a century as a symbol of democracy and has helped shape the democratic ideals of hundreds of thousands of leaders of public opinion—an accomplishment of the greatest significance to the Nation. Like the press, the school, and the church, it has fought for the freedom of the individual and has insisted upon his right to share in the Nation's cultural and spiritual heritage.

The publication of articles embodying the results of research in the *Library Quarterly,* in *College and Reference Libraries,* and to a less extent, in other library periodicals, has likewise been highly salutary. Its effect has been four-fold. It has familiarized librarians with the methods of research; it has stimulated investigation by practicing librarians and graduate students; it has helped convince scholars in other fields of the breadth and soundness of graduate study in librarianship; and it has filled the need which librarianship has long felt of reshaping and revitalizing its theory and practice in the light of new methods and discoveries.

The publication of long critical essays and carefully considered book reviews has exerted a comparable influence upon library literature. Criticism reflects a knowledge of standards and an ability to apply them, for the lack of which library literature long suffered to the detriment of its standing in the eyes of librarians generally and of members of other disciplines and professions. The ability to criticize intelligently gives proof of maturity in point of view and poise in judgment; when criticism is constructively applied, it insures not only a finer type of training for librarians, but improvement in performance and in the advancement of librarianship as a profession.

6.

Contributions to library literature from four other sources merit comment: (1) library schools (2) libraries which issue significant bulletins and occasional monographs (3) organizations which have established journals in related subject fields, and (4) individuals or organizations which have published compilations of resources for research or indexes or catalogs of special materials and collections.

The Graduate Library School of the University of Chicago has played a distinctive role as a library publisher. Reference has already been made to research studies in reading by Waples and Tyler and Gray and Monroe, and in other fields by other members of the School's staff which it has published. Comment has also been made on the part played by the *Library Quarterly* in stimulating research and criticism. In 1933, however, the School began the publication through the University of Chicago Press of *The University of Chicago Studies in Library Science*. To date it has issued 40 volumes in this series, 16 of which have contained the papers presented at its annual institutes which have been held since 1936. In all of the volumes, whether by members of its staff and alumni or by scholars and experts in other subjects, the School has undertaken to apply, when dealing with problems of librarianship, standards and methods of treatment similar to those applied to studies in other disciplines. The subjects treated have ranged from the history of mediaeval libraries and printing through the beginnings of libraries in New England, the South, and the Mid-West, down to the latest developments in the new but rapidly growing and tremendously important subject of communication. Certain titles stand out as landmarks in library study. Butler's *An Introduction to Library Science* and Joeckel's *The Government of the American Public Library* have attained the status of classics; and the volumes by Randall and Goodrich, in college library administration; of Joeckel and Carnovsky, in public library administration; and by Fussler, in microphotography, to mention three as representative, are constantly referred to by librarians everywhere.

The Columbia School of Library Service has likewise contributed notably through its syllabi on the subjects within its curriculum. *Living with Books,* by Haines, has become a classic in book selection, as has the *Guide to Reference Books* by Mudge and her successor, Winchell, all at one time of the Columbia School of Library Service or Library. Reece's works on education for librarianship have brought down to date the important developments since the Williamson *Report* of 1923, and the recent publications by Leigh, Bryan, and their associates growing out of the nation-wide Public Library Inquiry, have become *must* reading for all alert present and prospective librarians.

The Library School of the University of Illinois and the School of Librarianship of the University of California have published less extensively, but their publications in the field of education for librarianship have been challenging. *Library Trends,* a journal recently established at the University of Illinois and featuring the publication in a single issue of a number of articles on different aspects of a specific subject, and *The University of Illinois Contributions to Librarianship* have already established a significant place for themselves among library periodicals and monographs.

Publications by libraries throughout the Nation fall into different categories, though they are predominantly bibliographical or descriptive of special collections. They are indispensable for their humanistic content and supplement the subjects treated by the library schools concerned largely with phases of administration or education.

The *American Archivist* and the *Journal of American Documentation,* to mention two journals in special fields, are representations of new titles by fairly recent organizations, and, with the major surveys of library resources, with various union lists and catalogs, and with publication-wide indexes and catalogs, round out the field of library publication in the United States.

The impact of the study of these various publications from the social sciences and librarianship upon education for librarianship is vividly illustrated by two outlines I have developed over the years. The first was developed in the 1930's when I began offering a course on university library administration at the Graduate Library School of the University of Chicago which later grew into the volume by Wilson and Tauber entitled *The University Library*. In that course, by drawing upon the writings of Henri Fayol, Gulick and Urwick, and others, I developed a statement concerning the theory of administration in which the elements and principles of administration were set forth with brief definitions. The whole statement barely filled four typed pages, and all of it was drawn from fields other than the field of librarianship, and it was in a sense incidental or at most introductory to the course, the main body of which dealt with library practice. As I recall it, I devoted only one or two class periods to its consideration. Last week I concluded a course on the theory of library administration, the outline for which began with approximately the original four pages, but the body of which was drawn largely from publications written by librarians, which dealt theoretically and practically with elements and principles. Each publication presented a full-length study of organization, or planning, or staffing, or budgeting, or some other phase of administration, with practical situations and problems drawn from recent surveys of public and university libraries to give the subjects a specific basis of reality. The outline had grown from less than four pages to twenty-five, and the number of class periods from two to fifty, and the individual topics had acquired a range and comprehensiveness that was undreamed of by librarians a decade and a half earlier.

7.

The impact of the humanities upon the literature of librarianship during the past three decades, while less obvious than that of the social sciences, has nevertheless been significant. Just how significant, I cannot say. I cannot give a similar illustration showing the relation of cause and effect in the case of the humanities. I am not sufficiently familiar with literary criticism and the history of the arts and the literatures to see clearly what the relationship is between them and book selection and the book arts, nor am I able to trace the relationship between publications that deal with standards of value and appreciation on the one hand, and publications by librarians on the other, that apply their underlying principles to librarianship. But I am sure there is such a relationship, and that it is significant. James Harvey Robinson's *The Humanizing of Knowledge* (1923) written for scientists, and W. S. Learned's *The American Public Library and the Diffusion of Knowledge* (1924) pointed up the possibilities of contributions from the main stream of humanistic publications from which man has gained mental stimulation and aesthetic and spiritual insight. Books such as Butler's *An Introduction to Library Science* and Wellard's *Book Selection* showed how librarianship and book selection derived much of their motivation and standards of value from literature, the arts, philosophy, history, and the sciences as well as from the social sciences. This motivation and these standards have contributed to the broadening and deepening of the philosophy of librarianship upon which library service and adult education in America are firmly based. They emphasize the importance and dignity of the individual in a democratic society, an importance and dignity which must be maintained at all cost if men are to remain free.

Practical applications of this theory or philosophy have eventuated in a class of publications of great significance to librarians. *Living with Books,* by Haines; *How to Read a Book,* by Adler; *The Literature of Adult Education,* by Beals and Brady; *Books that Have Shaped the World,* by Eastman; *Classics of the Western World,* by Brown; and the "outlines" of history and literature and philosophy are but representative of the many titles of books about books, of bibliographies, and of special bulletins, handbooks, and treatises that enable librarians and library patrons to avail themselves of the ministry of the arts, philosophy, and literature. Publications of artists and musicians, of art museums and musical organizations, and of library associations in those fields, facilitate this work and lay open an inviting field of librarianship. The Great Books and to a less extent the American Heritage programs stem from this basic concept, as do those of libraries that loan reproductions from the fine arts and musical recordings or provide facilities for viewing notable pictures and listening to music reproduced by means of recordings or radio.

8.

The American Library School student cannot limit his professional reading to American publications since librarianship knows no national bounds. Like scholarship, it transcends national limitations and must concern itself with publications originating in other countries and dealing with foreign cultures. This fact I hardly need to emphasize here where you have only recently welcomed the return of your Dean after a year's study and association with European librarians. You have undoubtedly read this statement in the January 1953 A.L.A. *Bulletin* in which he wrote: "In areas of classification, cooperation, union catalog, documentation, library education, citizens advisory service, rural and urban public library service, and special library development, British librarianship compares very favorably with American librarianship." He might well have said the same of British library publications since they and the library publications of other countries likewise challenge the attention of the American library school student today. A half-dozen titles of major works in English, French, and German will illustrate this point: *The Library Association Record, The Year's Work in Librarianship, Bibliotheque de l'Ecole des Chartes, Handbuch der Bibliothekswissenschaft, Jahrbuch der deutschen Bibliotheken,* and *Zentralblatt für Bibliothekswesen*. Whether French, or German, or Italian, or Scandinavian, or Indian, or Japanese, they too are extensive and can broaden and deepen his understading of the role librarianship has played down through the centuries in conserving and transmitting the written record of man's priceless cultural heritage.

9.

This is the library literature, the library book shelf in outline upon which you as prospective librarians must draw for your professional preparation. These are the materials which you must master if you are to be fully informed about how the graphic records of man's past and present can be made to minister effectively to his present and future. This is the field in which you must carry on research and publish. You have already sensed how this material has broadened the scope of our training and laid the foundation for work leading to the M.A. and Ph.D. degrees. The library book shelf of 1923 could not support such curricula. But the book shelf of today, lengthened and enriched to a degree undreamed of three decades ago, makes such attainment possible. If it is supplemented and enriched by knowledge of related fields, it brings within your reach means by which you can prepare yourselves to enter upon a rich and significantly fruitful service to your fellow men.

AN AMERICAN LIBRARIAN'S HERITAGE*

WAYNE SHIRLEY

Dean, Library School, Pratt Institute

1.

At the Cleveland meeting of the American Library Association in June, 1950, I was asked to be a member of a Committee of Twelve to draw up a program for the celebration of the 75th Anniversary of the Association. Doubtless the invitation came to me as Chairman of the American Library History Round Table, an organization which your Dean and I have headed since its formation in 1946. Under the chairmanship of Dr. Ralph E. Ellsworth, the Committee drew up a program; just as many committees have done for similar anniversaries, but this program was different, for we agreed from the first that there was to be nothing antiquarian about our plans. Our program was to search the American heritage to find strength for the perils surrounding us in the present day world.

The American Heritage program is now well-known in the library world. There is a specialist at A.L.A.; libraries over the country have started such programs, and libraries will continue to start them. One such program was that of the Chattanooga Public Library, which I reported on as one of my committee assignments. I learned from this experience that the Program is good because it can be adapted to the locality where it is given. For instance, in Chattanooga, there is a unique arrangement about reading the Bible in public schools. Church and State are concepts difficult to grasp, but what goes on in Chattanooga's schools is a problem on which every Chattanoogan feels he has, or should have, an opinion. So I hope these programs continue to increase, for this is a great country, and we have variety enough to provide local material for the study of all our political and moral questions.

*A public lecture given at Florida State University, Tallahassee, May 4, 1953.

Thus it is that I am speaking to you on our heritage as American Librarians, for our profession is a part of America's heritage, and we may justly be proud that whatever else is said abroad about our institutions, American libraries are considered by all as something which is good, and as something they wish to have.

2.

We are what we are today because we are the heirs of our leaders who have gone before us, although in our case, we are rich in that a few of these pioneers are still with us. Herbert Putnam, for example. I heard him speak only two years ago, and I felt at the time the influence that comes from hearing a trail blazer. What a master he is at saying the right thing! A long list of anything gets pretty dull, including a long list of pioneers, so I shall speak only of five, each of whom I have chosen because I feel that each illustrates one of the characteristics which librarians either have or feel they should have.

First, of course, is Melville Dewey, 1851-1931, for we owe much to that master organizer and master promoter. A list of his accomplishments reads like an outline of a course in library administration; nor should it be forgotten that while he was doing these things for us he was organizing and promoting Simplified Spelling and Metric Reform for the rest of the world. Dewey gave us our most-used classification system, our schools for training librarians, our professional journals, our library supply organization, and our specialized services in many fields—travelling libraries for example. This man was a genius, and hence very troublesome, as I once heard Nicholas Murray Butler say, but he did have ideas, and he know how to get his ideas tried. Apparently Dewey cared little for what was in a book, but he did care much about getting books to everyone with the greatest possible efficiency. And since I am speaking to Florida librarians I should say that I have heard Dewey speak in the Albertson Public Library in Orlando. He was a master teller of tales to point a moral.

So from Dewey we get our drive to try things, whether

it be the American Heritage Program or charging books by sound. How Dewey would have loved the mechanisms we are developing to make our service faster and more accurate.

All librarians feel they must to some degree be scholars, even though most of us fall far short of this goal. The feeling for scholarship comes in direct descent from Justin Winsor, 1831-1897, the man who made us respectable by serving as President of A.L.A. for so many terms in the early days. He was known as a scholar, and his works still are basic in a study of American history. Dr. C. Seymour Thompson says of Winsor, "He was a man of great executive ability and qualities of leadership, and was a scholar."

Scholarship, then, may seem to be forgotten at library meetings, where so much time is taken up with public relations and with administration, but the regard and respect for scholarship still is there, and great respect is paid to librarians who have distinguished themselves as scholars as well. One thinks at once of Harry Miller Lydenberg, and the many fields of learning he has graced.

Another trait we feel all librarians should have is a love of literature, and an appreciation of good writing. Frances Clarke Sayers put it nicely in 1937 in her paper, "Lose not the Nightingale." Hence the pioneer I choose for this trait is Mary Wright Plummer, 1856-1916, who not only loved literature, but who could write herself. Here I speak with some authority, for Miss Plummer was a distinguished predecessor of mine and her framed photograph is behind my desk. She wrote much for the early Pratt Institute publications, all of which I have read to my enormous pleasure, for in those days all the world seemed young and beautiful, and "let's try it" was the motto. Perhaps some of you have been so fortunate as to read her *Seven Joys of Reading* which was printed in the *Sewanee Review*, Vol. 18, p. 454 ff., and which the H. W. Wilson Company later reprinted. This is one of the classics of librarianship, and is generally known, but few librarians know of Miss Plummer as a powerful as well as a finished writer. I am indebted to Anne Carroll Moore, one of Miss Plummer's students, for the following poem which was written about 1906 when the pogroms in Russia were at their worst.

THE CHOSEN PEOPLE.

> Thy chosen people, Lord! Aye, and for what?
>   Chosen to bear the world's contempt and scorn;
> Chosen to cringe and fawn, contrive and plot,
>   Only to win the right to live, being born;
> Chosen to bow the neck and bend the knee,
>   To hold the tongue when other tongues revile,
> To bear the burdens, bond-slaves e'en when free;
>   Give cheerfully, be spit upon and smile;
> Chosen for death, for torture and the screws,
>   While the slow centuries move, they say toward light!
> Lord, from the horrows of this endless night
>   Let us go free!—another people choose!

Who among us cannot be proud that a librarian could use words so powerfully?

And while I am speaking about librarians who could write, let me mention Edmund Lester Pearson, formerly Editor of The New York Public Library. His *Librarian at Play* is a book of essays on our trade which is so delightful all of us should give ourselves the pleasure of reading it.

A sense of order is characteristic of librarians; indeed, we have been accused by others of being too fond of our housekeeping, and voices among us have said that we were too fond of having everything in its place. Too often we speak of some reader interrupting us when we are doing something, which surely is getting first things last. The famous story illustrating this point is of the Harvard librarian who knew where every book was except one, and he was going out to get that one as he was locking up. Mr. Keyes Metcalf, the present Harvard librarian, told me this tale is true.

I have always thought the source of this feeling for order was Charles Ammi Cutter, 1837-1903, a great librarian and a great scholar. His great work was the *Catalog* of the Boston Atheneum and from his experience in compiling this *Catalog* he drew up his *Rules for a Dictionary Catalog*, which is the foundation of our cataloging and classification today. Also we know him as the man who devised our Cutter Numbers. His classification scheme, called the Expansive Classification, is not so well known, since it is used in few libraries today. Cutter was so much a scholar he never finished the system, as he was always perfecting it, even though one of his contemporaries said that when used by a large library "botany ran up through the stacks like a tree." This system is still in use at Forbes Library at Northampton, Massachusetts, where Cutter once was librarian. Josephine Adams Rathbone used to repeat the remark about botany to her students and she never failed to say also, "And he was a wonderful dancer." Perhaps we owe to Cutter our predilection for square dances which have become a feature of so many library meetings.

John Cotton Dana, 1865-1929, was trained as a lawyer, and indeed he did practice for a while, but he soon went into libraries. He served as librarian in Denver and Springfield, Massachusetts, but he is chiefly known as the librarian of the Free Public Library of Newark, New Jersey. We owe to Dana our urge to tell the world about ourselves. He seized any means at hand to do this from billboards to after-luncheon talks at service clubs. He thoroughly enjoyed telling the profession precisely how he felt on any matter, and if a number of toes were stepped on in the telling so much the better. "A blast from Mr. Dana" was one of the pleasures librarians looked for during many years.

We owe to Dana also the idea of special libraries, and the founding of the Special Libraries Association in 1910. The library world, then and now, were and are of two opinions as to the value of this contribution. Some consider Dana's action in this matter as a divisive force, and their argument is reinforced by the fact that the Special Libraries Association has no connection with the American Library Association. Others will argue as strongly that he made libraries a force in an era where they had not been generally established. There may be arguments on this point, but there is general agreement that he taught us that it is a part of our jobs to tell our story to the world.

There are other pioneers, of course, and books are being written about them under the leadership of Mrs. Emily Miller Danton, but until these books appear, a short survey is available in the March 15, 1951 *Library Journal* under the title of "A Library Hall of Fame." The *Library Journal* did not include Mr. R. R. Bowker, because he was not a librarian, and because he was one of the founders of the *Journal*, even though the librarians present, among whom was myself, urged the *Journal* editors to do so. Hence it seems only proper that I should say something of him. I heard Mr. Bowker speak in 1928, when he was old and blind, but his great charm of manner easily overcame these handicaps. He was the person who kept things on an even keel in the early days, and what ability he must have had to keep the peace among such men as Dana, Dewey, and Poole, all of whom were certain that they were right, and all of whom delighted in stating their feelings in the strongest possible language.

3.

Now to go from remarks on individual pioneers to the ideas which we follow. Perhaps philosophy is a better word, as we are told a philosophy of librarianship is one of our greatest needs, but I am not the one to set forth such a statement of belief since I do not feel this need. I shall instead talk about eight ideas which I believe are fundamental to our way of life.

First, however, I should tell you what I consider the basic statement for the operation of libraries today. This is found in a Report of the Trustees of the Boston Public Library to the Common Council of that city dated July 6, 1852. This Report was written by a subcommittee of the Trustees among whom were Edward Everett and George Ticknor. The sections which follow were written by Ticknor:

> Still, certain points seem to rise up with so much prominence, that without deciding on any formal arrangement, until experience shall show what is practically useful—we may perhaps foresee that such a library as is contemplated would naturally fall into four classes, viz:
> I. *Books that cannot be taken out of the Library*, such as Cyclopedias, Dictionaries, important public documents and books. . . .
> II. *Books that few persons will wish to read*, and of which, therefore, only one copy will be kept. . . .
> III. *Books that will be often asked for* . . . of which copies should be provided in such numbers that many persons . . . can be reading the same work at the same moment, and so render . . . the literature of the day accessible to the whole people at the only time they care for it,—that is, when it is living, fresh and new. . . .
> IV. Periodicals. . . .

All four points are important, but the most important is

three, for in that section is the basis of the public library as we know it. Edward Everett had argued for a scholars' library, a reference library as we would say today, but the Report was adopted and Ticknor won. This was doubly interesting, for Ticknor was a Spanish scholar of great repute. His cousin William Davis Ticknor was the bookseller and publisher, so Ticknor was not influenced by his business to take this position.

4.

A heritage must not be thought of only as the inheritance of what is good, or what is strong. All of us carry through life the weak as well, and this is true of institutions also, so I shall speak first of two of our weaknesses, and then go on to happier matters.

The first is our love of gadgetry. If you wish to have a good understanding of this, read through the early volumes of the *Library Journal.* I shall start with the Founding Fathers. Dewey loved efficiency so much he would go to great lengths to attain it. One way was to shorten names, so he started with himself. He began life as Melville Louis Kossuth Dewey. First he dropped the Kossuth and then the Louis. Then he shortened the Melville to Melvil and the Dewey to Dui. He ended up as Dewey. Another example: It was felt that common names as Charles should be spelled by some sort of symbol, so Charles Ammi Cutter became C: Cutter, and you will find articles in the *Journal* signed by him in this fashion. Cutter Numbers were an invention. C: was a gadget. Another example L: was to stand for Lewis, Louis, Ludwig, Luigi, Luis, and *Louisa* and *Louise,* to give an example of a scheme guaranteed to unseat a cataloger's reason.

A well-known New England librarian believed that sloping the bottom shelves in our bookcases would solve most of our problems, and he was only too happy to tell others of his faith. These shelves doubtless were good and most of us use them today, but he went even further by shelving his books in a reverse order, that is, from the bottom to the top of the case, and from right to left on the shelf. Finding a book in that library really was something!

But I save the finest example of this pseudo-efficiency for my own library. It was felt some years ago that the Zero in the Dewey class beginning with that number could be omitted "since everybody knew what it meant." Hence, if a bibliography had the number 016.743, the back of the book would be marked 16.743, and as a result such books were shelved as a rule in 167.43, for decimal points mean little to pages, particularly in dark corners. My point is that time savers are to be used with care, since only too often their use means that succeeding librarians have a snarl to unravel .

A second weakness is our dreadful professional terminology. If a person tried, he would have difficulty to find words so uninspiring as those we use every day—words as circulation, reference, shelflist, accession, assistant, borrower, adult education, work with young people, work with the foreign born. Some of these terms are being displaced, but the new words are little better. Work with the foreign born is now "intercultural activities," for example. We should take a leaf from the book of the children who come to us, for they come to the desk and tell us they "want to join the library." There's good English, which expresses an appealing idea in pleasing words, words rich in association.

Doubtless we have other weaknesses of a congenital character, but let's not dwell too much on the weaknesses and go on to speak about some of the strengths of our heritage.

5.

One great strength is our belief in the value of personality. True, this seems to be sapped to a degree by the increasing use of classification systems, where a person is to be sought who will fit into the Procrustean bed of some job description, but this has not gone too far. We still profit from the librarians who sought out strong people with the confidence that these persons would make their own jobs, and that they would advance librarianship by being given opportunity to show what they could do. One of the leaders in this school of thought was W. H. Brett of Cleveland. He used to go to library conferences to search out strong people to hire for Cleveland. He would find something for them to do after they got there, and look at the magnificent Cleveland system of today! Another was E. H. Anderson. He was always on the watch, particularly for able young men, so that The New York Public Library became the training ground for many of the great librarians of America, and it was so recognized in and out of the field. The opinion of the Library is still sought when some important post is to be filled, and for years it seemed as if everyone in a position of some responsibility had worked at the New York Public. Your Dean is such a person, and I am proud to be of this group also. This year's A.L.A. Presidential candidates are two others. The A.L.A. Executive Secretary is a fifth.

Another benefit we reap from this heritage is that the librarians will give an accurate opinion of other librarians, particularly those new in the field. I do not think that librarians are harsher than others in judging people, but we do realize that everyone has weak points, and we are willing to go on record to that effect. This is not generally true, as other groups are good at stating only the strong points of a person. To find the whole picture, one has to read between, above, and below the lines. This also is being broken down, but it is still possible to hear a librarian speak of a beginner as a "weak" or as a "strong" person. Indeed the State of New York recognizes this state of affairs, for in order to qualify for a license as a professional public librarian in New York it is necessary to work two years, and to submit the opinion of one's librarian on one's professional abilities. This is in addition to library school graduation and to passing a professional examination.

We believe in the organized library movement, and we back up our belief by serving on committees, each of which takes as its responsibility some small segment of librarianship. Always someone can be found to work on the bread and butter committees such as Library Binding and Insurance, as opposed to committees which labor in the limelight as Federal Relations or Personnel. This dividing up of the field has resulted in a library system which all the world admires and copies to some extent, and you can be proud that the efforts of librarians who were once students as yourselves have left you this successful mechanism which it will be yours to improve. Some day at meetings you will hear a librarian say that he must be about his "A.L.A. chores" and you will know that this person, along with either two or four others, is trying to advance librarianship in one small area.

This is the time to pay tribute to Dr. Charles H. Brown, the distinguished bibliographer on this campus a year ago and lecturer this year, for it is due to his political insight and his effort to learn the thought of others on the subject, that we have an A.L.A. which is based on divisional membership. This device of joint membership functions precisely as our Federal and our State citizenship, and it has only begun to bring its weight to bear on our problems. It is, however, hard on the budget, for now the Divisions all have so much money they *all* publish a periodical we must buy.

We believe in cooperation. The earliest example was even international, for the *Library Journal* was to serve as the official organ of the British Library Association and of the American Library Association, but this was too much of a load for even so good an idea as cooperation. Another early example was cooperative action to get out the periodical and other indexes. Present examples are the various Union Catalogs, Library Centers, Cooperative Storage, and intercollegiate corporations to further library cooperation. The Farmington Plan is another. Libraries spend hours of staff time in checking periodical holdings so that all libraries can know of our holdings, and thus is developed a network of interlibrary loans which makes most of the periodicals of the country available on demand. In short, we work together, and we compete only in the purchase of rarities which tickle our personal or professional vanity, but then after we get them, we lend these also.

One of our strongest beliefs, and one which should give us the greatest happiness, even though now and again it leads us to make ridiculous statements, is our belief that libraries are good, not just good, but good in the sense of being counteracting forces to the evils which afflict mankind. At various times libraries have been thought capable of keeping young men out of saloons, of protecting mill girls from temptations of the city, and of strengthening our morals in other ways.

Libraries are considered a comfort for the lonely, as mechanisms for those who want to get ahead—as Barrie recognized— and as restoratives for those in trouble. In short, they have been and are, recommended as curatives for all the afflictions with which man is visited. This is true. In fact there is one Book in itself which has done and is doing all these services for us. The classic example of the feeling that books are good is the battle for Sunday opening of libraries, the account of which you will enjoy reading. Books won, but they lost in their turn when it became too costly to keep the libraries open.

Of late we have been told we should spurn all feeling for the missionary spirit. It seems to me indeed rash to push aside a force which has changed the world, but if we must cast aside this great power, let us pause for a while to pay a tribute to those who were moved by their belief in libraries. Their names are legion and the roll is still growing. I heard a librarian, who serves a State near your own, speak only last summer of her pleasure when a county official backed libraries because they were good for the children, even though he himself could not write his own name.

So may I tell you about Miss E. Louise Jones of the Massachusetts Library Commission, who by the way is still living, as typical of that devoted group of single women who established so many libraries in this country. May I be permitted a personal note to make my point.

My mother was left a widow with three children to support, and shortly after her husband's death she was given the library in a small New Hampshire city. Of course these days, we turn our faces in horror from anything so unprofessional, but it did happen, and my mother was a good librarian. I began my library career, as I like to tell my students, by stamping books at the age of seven. At any rate, my mother wrote to Miss Jones, and this official of another State came to help her start her library. I remember the visit vividly, for we had oranges for supper the night when Miss Jones came to our house. This is a joke now, but oranges in New Hampshire in 1907 *were* a treat. I can see how they looked on the table even today.

One of our cynics said in 1878 "the librarian who reads is lost," and it is said now and again by our sophisticates. This saying is in reality a defense mechanism for the man who is in the wrong job, for the truth is that the librarian who does *not* read is lost. Josephine Adams Rathbone used to say that a librarian who did not enjoy reading his professional literature was in the wrong profession. This is indeed Spartan doctrine, but any of us who does not enjoy reading is in the wrong job. J. N. Larned, like Winsor, a scholar and a librarian, defined study as having "some special cultivation of mind or some particular acquisition in view." He defined reading as "the pursuit of good that is in books." Before saying this, Larned had warned that books are like baskets; of slight interest in themselves, but of great interest and of great difference of value according to their contents. Our rare book men will say that Larned is going too far when he rules out an interest in books regardless of content.

We spend our lives among shelves of books, and soon all libraries begin to look alike, the only difference being that some have more books. The longer we stay in the field, however, the more books mean to us. I sometime feel that we can tell the worth of books by looking at their backs, but this may be claiming too much. We do not have to read all books, nor do I feel it necessary that we should wish to do so, but I do feel that a love of reading is basic in our heritage.

Perhaps I may digress a bit to tell you about good and bad books. First I shall pass on to you the advice given my mother by one of America's great book men, Harry Thurston Peck. He was vacationing in my home town, and my mother asked him about discarding an old encyclopedia. He said, "Young woman, if a book was good in the first place, it will be good again." May I venture some advice of my own. Any autobiography which has a photograph of the author as a frontispiece with the words "yours truly, the Author" written on it is not a good book, and any book which says it is "the truth" about anything or any person should be suspect at once.

So the librarian who reads is not lost. He is a man who has found his profession. Listen when you hear librarians talking, and you will hear someone who is about to retire say, "At last, time enough to read." As a rule he will read only at spare moments, and he will keep on working in the field which has made his life so worth while. Messrs. Charles H. Brown, Joseph E. Wheeler, and H. M. Lydenberg are fine examples of this post-retirement activity.

And now for the last, and the greatest item in our heritage. We believe in freedom. We believe every book should have its chance, and that no book should be denied its right to claim whatever place it can hold in the world's thinking or the world's memory. Let me state at once that this does not mean in the least that we must defend every book, far from it. If we think a book is bad, we should not feel that we are denying freedom if we do not buy it. What we do need to defend is our right at all times to choose among all books and it is then up to us to strengthen ourselves so the books we buy are good books, by which I mean worth while books. Margaret Scoggin says in the November 1952 A.L.A. *Bulletin* that "book selection is a test of ourselves." That is why it is good to meet and to talk over with other librarians in the same field, so that we can check on our prejudices lest they grow too powerful.

We believe in freedom of choice among books, both as individuals, and as men and women organized in a profession. Our Library Bill of Rights is a charter which tells us that we do not stand alone. We are against censorship. We are against labeling. And we are against having any group in a community say what other groups shall read. Substitute individual for "group" in the preceding sentence and it still stands.

I wish I could stand here as a doughty battler for freedom for books and as one who has fought the good fight and lost or won, but alas, I cannot do so. In my libraries I have been allowed to buy as I thought best, and no questions have ever been asked, but I like to think of what Arthur Garfield Hayes said at A.L.A. in Cincinnati in 1940 when someone asked him what he would do if he were a librarian and some powerful individual or group told him he could not buy a certain book. He said, "I do not know what I would do, but I do know what I should do." We know what we ought to do, and as a rule we meet the test. Our serious fault in such matters is a tendency to assume that those who differ with us are not also persons of integrity.

These, then, seem to me to be our birthright, but before I go on to speak of our heritage as Americans I do want to give you a statement of Charles A. Cutter's which seems to me to be the most inclusive statement of library possibilities I have read anywhere. Cutter said he wanted a system which would make it possible "to lend anything to anybody in any desired quantity for any desired length of time." This is indeed a spacious vineyard in which to labor, and I hope that each of you finds his particular vine which he will cause to grow great by the labor, thought, and love he expends in caring for its growth and nurture.

6.

And now to close my remarks by speaking to you about our heritage as Americans. Many of you will recall the passage from the Bible which says that Jesus "taught them as one having authority and not as a scribe." Do I speak to you as one having authority? The answer is "No," but the main point is that no one can do this, for only we ourselves can tell us what we must do or what we must be to be Americans. That is a burden *we* must bear, and a responsibility we cannot shirk. Others may only suggest what our heritage as Americans is, and since I have the floor at the moment, here are my suggestions.

First of all we must remember that we participate in the experiments of government of forty-eight States, for our Constitution says that each State must grant "full faith and credit" to the laws of the other States. That is one of our great sources of strength, for we can observe the results of this great governmental experimental laboratory, and copy what is good, and avoid what is bad. Equally we can copy the bad and avoid what is good, for there is nothing in freedom to guarantee that we choose the better way.

Then we must remember that our government is based on the assumption that each one of us is significant. We believe that each one of us was made in the image of God, and so attention must be paid to us, no matter how unimportant we may seem to be in the world's affairs. We do not have the restful experience of life in a totalitarian state where we are told what we shall do and what we shall think. Our way is harder; we must choose, and we pay a heavy price of responsibility for this freedom to choose. Each American can stake out his claim for his place in the world and then he can try to prove it.

In New York we have each year "I am an American Day." This may seem strange to you, for most of the people you know are Americans and have been for generations, but it is not so in New York. There, the vast majority are the children of parents born abroad, and there are also large numbers born abroad themselves. Our present Mayor was born in Italy, and his predecessor was born in Ireland. So "I am an American Day" is now well established in New York, and crowds of over 1,000,000 have attended. The speakers for these observances are all famous men, but the talks which have grown greatest as time goes on were those given by Judge Learned Hand in 1944 and 1945. In 1944 he said, "The spirit of liberty is that spirit which is not too sure that it is right; which seems to understand the minds of other men and women; which weighs their interests alongside its own without bias; which remembers that not even a sparrow falls to earth unheeded; the spirit of Him whose pitiless and difficult doctrine of self-abandonment and self-forgetfulness we can neither disregard, nor yet bring ourselves to obey." In 1945 he said, "Should mankind be divided between those who use others at their will and those who must submit; whether the measure of a man's power to shape his own destiny should be the force at his disposal? Our nation was founded on the answer to these questions."

Three more quotations and I am done: Gerald W. Johnson says "To be American requires thought, effort, and, especially courage." Judge Hand asks, "For how long are we safe, and how far have we removed our peril? If we could not exist as a nation half slave and half free, are we sure that we can exist in a world half slave and half free?" We do not know, but I for one shall remember what Gilbert E. Govan, a librarian like ourselves wrote: We can stand "steady in our shoes with typical American faith in ourselves and in our future."